A REVERENCE for WOOD

ERIC SLOANE

DOVER PUBLICATIONS, INC.
Mineola, New York

To Joseph McLaughlin
the man at my publishers' office who
insisted upon my doing this book

Copyright

Copyright © 1965 by Wilfred Funk, Inc.
All rights reserved.

Bibliographical Note

This Dover edition, first published in 2004, is an unabridged republication of the work originally published by Funk & Wagnalls, New York in 1965.

Library of Congress Cataloging-in-Publication Data

Sloane, Eric.
    A reverence for wood / Eric Sloane.
        p. cm.
    Reprint. Originally published: New York : Funk & Wagnalls, 1965.
    ISBN 0-486-43394-3 (pbk.)
    1. Wood. 2. Woodwork—United States—History. 3. Carpentry—United States—History. I. Title.
TA419.S583 2004
620.1'2—dc22

2003064606

Manufactured in the United States of America
Dover Publications, Inc., 31 East 2nd Street, Mineola, N.Y. 11501

CONTENTS

AUTHOR'S NOTE

The way this book came about, as I think back on it, is an odd one. For after having done a score of books about early American life, I found that I'd never done the one I first had in mind, the book to be called *A Reverence for Wood*.

As a painter of clouds and sky, my greater interests were in flying and in meteorology. I believe I was the first weatherman on television; I built the Hall of Atmosphere in the American Museum of Natural History (Willetts Memorial) in 1945, and later I wrote several books about weather. When World War II came along I did manuals and three dimensional models of weather phenomena for military flyers. The more research I did in meteorology, the more impressed I became with the weather knowledge of the early American. I found an amazing source of information in old diaries and almanacs, and before long my own interests in weather became submerged in the lore of the early American countryman. His manner of living with the seasons instead of battling to overcome them, his regard for natural resources, and his amazing reverence for wood seemed to be worth recording.

I was recalling this to my friend Hugh Weidinger one day as we were flying over the New England countryside. "Some day soon," I said, "I must do the book about trees and wood." Down below, the wooded hills were just turning to their autumn colors, and the shadow of our plane raced across a sea of crimson and russet.

"You'd better write it soon, while there are some trees left," said Hugh. "Look ahead." He pointed over the nose of the plane.

There on the horizon began the mathematical pattern of the metropolis. Fifty miles from its center, New York City had spilled rudely over the design of nature. It was obvious that wherever such an intrusion had taken place, there would never be a going back. Nothing can take over as completely as man: he has had many complex relationships with the forest in the course of history, but where solid concrete appears, those relationships seem to end and man's dominance becomes complete.

"You just must admit it," my friend said. "Trees and wood are on their way out. Everything is metal and plastic these days. Look at this airplane; it's not made of wood the way planes once were."

It was something to think about as we roared on. But I then realized that we were running on wood fuel! The gasoline that operated our engine came from prehistoric forests that had grown and perished when there were no men and no need for conservation.

Sometimes even I have been trapped by the illusion that the uses of wood are declining, and on one of my infrequent trips to New York, a glance around the city revealed the vast changes made there within the last ten years. What impact, I thought, could a book about trees and wood have on people living in this world of concrete and glass and steel?

Certainly we don't see as much wood as we once did, yet wood is still with us. I realized that the very contract for my book was made of materials derived from wood. Every time one picks up the telephone to call long distance, one's voice is conveyed across the country by hundreds of miles of wires strung from wooden post to wooden post; even the number you call is listed in a directory made entirely of wood pulp. We think of traveling by "railroad," yet there is far more wood in the ties than there is steel in the rails. Modern tires, plastics, medicines and paints, boxes and cartons and bags and newspapers; almost everything we use can still be traced in some way to the tree. The pencil (and its eraser) and the paper on which I am writing this book, the ink and the paints that I use to illustrate it, all are wood products. The finished book you are now reading began as a tree. My royalty checks and the envelopes they arrive in will also be wood products.

I just read in a newspaper that because of plastics and other innovations, the usefulness of the tree has diminished in the past half century. But the same newspaper (which boasts the country's largest circulation) enjoys the products of the forest; each Sunday issue destroys a sizeable grove.

It may be that after we have spent a century or two in expending our wealth of wood to seek the riches of other planets, we will realize that our greatest wealth was right here on earth after all.

I derive a certain pleasure from an awareness of our gift of wood. Besides giving me its chemical and utilitarian benefits, like the fireplace that "warms the soul as well as the body," the tree and its wood are a most necessary part of my life's aesthetic enjoyment.

Perhaps after reading this book when you hear the rustling of leaves or the wind in the boughs, smell the fragrance of a Christmas tree or the burning of a pine log in the fireplace, or see the majesty of a gnarled and ancient oak, you will revive some faint memory from our early American heritage and share with those first settlers a reverence for wood.

Eric Sloane

Weather Hill Farm
Cornwall Bridge
Connecticut

Postscript: The names and dates and places in the following story have been given accurately to the best of my ability; yet my writing is supposed to be a tale, and as in any historical novel, my own imagination has blended with fact to create poetical reality.

Radial sections of Typical American Woods *

*See inside front cover.

Perpetual modernness is the measure of merit in every work of art.
Emerson

The Old Barn

"They don't build them like that now," said Harley as he tapped his wrecking bar against one of the old pegged joints.

I was above on a ladder, ready to tackle the roof. It seemed wrong to destroy such symmetry. The ancient shingles lay haphazardly like matted grass on a hill, but from my vantage point, the wooden roof pattern stretched away with a mathematical grace that first became part of the local landscape, then of the distant horizon. Sighting along the peak I could see wavy contours that indicated the position of each rafter underneath. Old barn roofs always have a lively style and no two will settle in the same way. The long tobacco barns of Connecticut, after a century of weather, begin to slouch comfortably into the contours of the land upon which they rest. The stone barns of Pennsylvania have rigid walls, which support their roof peaks in a fairly straight posture for a number of years; then, after a brief period of picturesque decay, the middle rafters weaken, and under the weight of wet snow one certain winter night, the whole covering falls at once into the barn's deserted innards.

It is said that the reason wooden roofs on stone barns collapse is that after some two centuries of drying, the whole wooden roof shrinks. While stone sides stay put, a vast stretch of wooden roof will actually become inches smaller in a century. The thought of a barn becoming smaller with age seems strange, but such shrinkage is nevertheless plainly measurable.

Like most of the very early American buildings, my barn roof had no rooftree (that board which runs the length of the peak, also known as a *ridgepole* or *ridge rafter*). Each pair of slanting rafters was merely pegged together at the peak and held in place by wide chestnut roof boards. Now, after some hundred winters had imposed their pressing weight, the roofing lay loosely over the rafters like a big soft gray tapestry.

When you tear down an old barn, you begin at the top, and the shingles are always first to go. Harley had explained that to me.

"There's a right way to do things and a wrong way," he said. "Then there's the quick way. That's how city folks like to work, so it costs them most in the long run."

The current method of tearing down barns is by bulldozer and wire cable. But since the old mortised joints are usually stronger than the whole lengths of beam, when a barn is pulled down in this way, good wood splits. The roof then falls like a sodden cape over the whole thing, and demolition becomes harder and takes longer. So I chose the seemingly slower old-time method; I started by removing the roof.

I found that the greenish hue of old roof shingles comes from actual moss, and that rather than causing rot, moss often preserves a roof. It adds to the shingle's ability to "breathe," to swell quickly during a shower, thereby closing each crack or hole. There are old barn roofs through which you can see the stars, yet which won't leak in a hard rainstorm.

Most architectural historians tell us that the fronts of many old buildings were constructed of clapboard, while the backs were shingled. "It was a matter of fashion," they explain. "Shingles were just not fashionable." They forget how weather-minded and wood-wise early builders were—they usually placed the back of a building to the north, where the cold wet winds hit, and for this side they chose cedar shingles simply for greater protection.

Virgin American white cedarwood had a remarkable quality to resist water and damp-rot. During the 1700's, most of the nation's shingle material came from the New Jersey cedar swamps. The demand was so great that by the 1800's these swamplands were depleted of their trees. After that, astonishingly enough, white cedar was *mined* in New Jersey. It was while a stump was being removed from these swamps that several sunken logs were loosened and floated to the surface. The logs had been submerged anywhere from a few centuries to a thousand years!

IRON PROGUE
MUD-HORSE

When the depleted cedar swamps were mined
for
buried white cedar
which was raised and sawed into blocks

MAUL
FROE
3 ft

then "rived" into shingle slabs.
Shingles were finished on a Shaving Horse
with a drawknife

These submerged logs, it was found, were of a superior quality and contained good timber. It was further discovered that a layer of fallen cedar trunks, about twelve feet deep, covered the swamp bottom. When people learned of the remarkable lightness and durability of this material, there was a great demand for it. With the aid of an iron "progue pin," to probe beneath the surface of the water and locate the sunken logs, *cedar mining* prospered until the Civil War.

The roof on Independence Hall in Philadelphia was made of this material, and many of the three-foot shingles on historic American homes are from cedar that had been buried under the water for centuries.

One might not notice it from the ground, but any ancient shingled roof is usually studded with thousands of nails that have pushed outward from the shingles like quills on a porcupine. The reason for this is interesting, for it demonstrates how softwoods tend to breathe with every atmospheric change. Each wetting and drying, heating and cooling, each pressure change of new weather, will bring about some tiny expansion or contraction. At a twice-a-day minimum, in fifty years, this phenomenon will produce about thirty thousand movements, each of which tends to squeeze the old nails out of the softwood. Square nails have more surface area (with that much more friction) and so they do resist more than round nails.

"It's too bad," I remarked, "the way these nails pull out of the shingles. I guess the old-timers didn't figure on that."

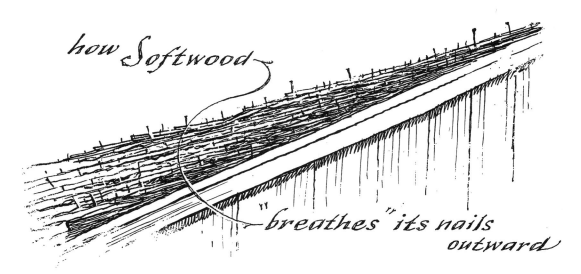

how Softwood

"breathes" its nails outward

"We always left them that way on purpose," said Harley. "It kept the snow in place."

"Snow in place? You wanted the snow to *stay* there?"

"Sure," he replied. "To keep the heat in. Most barn heat goes out the roof, doesn't it? Warmest thing we have up here in Warren during February is the snow."

I'm not sure he really meant that, but I do recall being able to pick out all the lived-in homes and barns along the road just by observing the amount of snow on their roofs. An abandoned barn will usually keep its blanket of snow right on into spring. There's an old New England saying—"what with the high cost of heating, the average icicle on a roof costs about five dollars a foot." Indeed, it does cost about that much to melt off roof snow into freezing icicles at the eaves.

Snow, in the early days, was a cherished thing, not the nuisance that we now consider it. Far from being removed from a highway, snow was actually placed on the roads. It was even shoveled onto the old covered bridges. Then it was packed down with snow-rollers to make the only really smooth highways of that time. Sometimes when snow was scarce, it was transported from the forest and spread on the roads. People used to pile cornstalks around the foundation of a house or a barn just to hold the snow there. It kept the winter wind out. They put little spikes and iron eagles with outstretched wings on their roofs, not so much to keep the ice from falling on passers-by as to keep a good blanket of snow there. So I suppose a roughly shingled roof or one with its nails protruding also held the snow in place.

"I'm saving all the wrought nails," I called down to Harley. "Put them in a box. They sell for three cents apiece, you know."

The fact that he didn't reply was no indication of his not having heard. Or that he had no opinion. Why anyone would collect old nails when he could afford good store nails was too upsetting a subject for him to discuss. He once asked me why I like wormy chestnut, yet throw away clothing with moth holes in it. I cause him much wonderment. And as for my making frames for my paintings from "miserable old weathered boards full of knots and decay—he'll just never understand that.

Even to me, for a while, the idea of old worn barn wood for picture framing seemed a bit affected. But the beauty of naturally aged wood has a strong appeal to the human mind. I decided also that its abstract pattern of natural decay is really more pleasing than anything solely ornamental that a frame-maker might concoct. If a frame is part of a painting (and it usually is), choosing the frame should be the important final touch of the painter himself. So my love affair with old wood won out.

Strangely enough, however, wood that is exposed to the weather and the seasons for a long time becomes too "athletic." It seems to get accustomed to the strong breathing caused by atmospheric changes. Barn siding, for example, when removed to the steady dry atmosphere indoors, will exhibit a most remarkable shrinkage. Mitered frame corners will soon pull apart, and wall sheathing will separate a full inch. Because of this, I adopted the foolproof early American "ship-lap" or lapped joint for all my frames, and I still wonder why this simple and strongest of joints is not used more today.

How the SHIP·LAP *frame is made.*

a *Mitered joint* tends to dry apart, a *Ship·lap* stays.

Another old-time feature I have revived is painting on wood. Actually I use a *composition wood*, called Masonite; yet it is very similar to the base used by many early American painters, a flat piece of smooth tight-grained wood. While canvas absorbs dampness from the atmosphere, becoming first limp then taut (causing the crackle that appears in most ancient paintings), hardwood when painted on both sides has a minimum of expansion and contraction.

It would surprise most people to learn how many of our famous early American "canvases" were really paintings done on slabs of wood. Many traveling portrait painters and limners of the 1700's carried stacks of wood panels with them instead of canvas and stretchers, and they were expert at knowing the woods which are least likely to crack, warp, or be affected by moisture. The Peale family of artists, it is said, imported slabs of wood from Europe, much older and dryer than any native American wood.

In 1925, when I met a disgruntled lumber salesman who gave me all his samples of "a new building board," I was the first to try them out as a surface on which to paint pictures. Now, forty years later, about half of all the work of contemporary American artists is done on such composition board. And there's even less warping or shrinking in composition board than there is in plain wood, for there are no pores or grain to harbor dampness.

The surface of the average large antique pine table might change its width by a quarter-inch between midsummer and midwinter! The end clamp-boards, of course, will not change their *length* much, because wood shrinks more *across* the grain than *with* the grain (the difference is more than ten to one). Instead of clamp-boards, *dovetail keys* were sometimes slid into place, strengthening a panel without the use of nails or screws, yet giving the panel leeway to expand or contract.

Bowls, too, unless they are made of root or burl grain, will shrink across the grain with advanced age: the older they get, the more oval they become. The wide floorboards in ancient houses that pull apart and often let you see into the room below are also examples of how woods (like human beings) shrink in old age.

As Harley removed each piece of siding, he leaned it upright against the barn to keep it dry.

"They'll curve up if you lay them flat on the ground," he said.

It is significant that the old barn boards had kept straight for over a

The *shrinking* of wood when drying, may be seen in a *clamped** table-top

CLAMP·BOARD*

WHICH WILL SHRINK DURING WINTER
AND SWELL DURING THE MOIST SUMMER.

Pine

Winter
Shrink

Summer
Swell

..or with wooden-pegged furniture after a century of drying.

pegs often protrude

PINE

.. or how round wooden bowls become oval with age.

shrinking
across the
grain

new
in
1765

and
1965

.. or the wide
spaces between floorboards and in panels.

Loosely nailed cellar strips

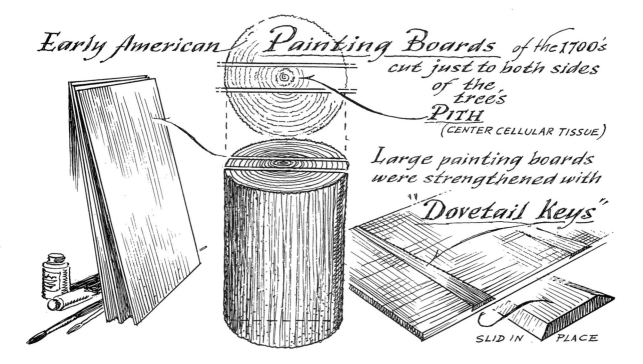

Early American **Painting Boards** *of the 1700's cut just to both sides of the tree's* PITH (CENTER CELLULAR TISSUE)

Large painting boards were strengthened with "**Dovetail Keys**"

SLID IN PLACE

century when in place, yet were still prey to distortion the moment they were removed and exposed to uneven drying.

Uneven drying causes warp. That is why I paint both sides of my painting boards, so the entire piece of wood will dry evenly. With one side working against the other, there can be no warp. A board left in the grass will be pushed by the dampness of the ground into a saucerlike shape. Just turn it over and in a day or so the process will recur in the opposite direction. By wetting the top side of a sheet of paper, you can see instantly how this works. I have pictured warp in unseasoned timber with purposely exaggerated drawings, showing that some parts dry and shrink more than others because the grain has forced them to do so.

"Well, there's a scaffold for you!" Harley called out as he hit a last nail five good whacks. The last whack glanced off the nail head and struck the base wood.

"Four times out of five is a good average," I remarked.

"Used to do it six times out of five," he said.

Yankee humor, I thought, but I'll go along with it.

the Anatomy of WOOD WARPAGE

Moisture (or lack of it) causes warp.

Ⓐ   Ⓑ

DRYING BY SUN'S
HEAT, CAUSING
SHRINKAGE Ⓑ

DAMP
GRASS

SWELLING CAUSED
BY DAMPNESS Ⓐ

Turn the board over
and it will unwarp.

... but most warping in today's lumber is from Seasoning Shrinking

ANNUAL
RINGS

here's how board shrinks

Ⓑ

Ⓐ

Ⓒ

Ⓐ SHRINKS IN
THICKNESS

Ⓑ OUT-OF-SQUARE
WARPAGE

Ⓒ WARPS
TWO WAYS

Wetting the concave side

HOT WATER

then weighting it,
will usually
straighten
a warped
board

DAMP UNDERSIDE

Reversing a board is another remedy.

HEART SIDE ALL ONE WAY, CAUSING
SCALLOPED CONTOUR

HEART SIDES NOW ALTERNATING
MAKES A SMOOTHER SURFACE

Uneven drying / *Uneven wetting* = *uneven shrinkage ∴ warping*

"So I give up. How did you manage that?"

"Worked overtime," he said.

He attacked another piece of siding with his wrecking bar, making a solid bite, then pushed the board out and away. There was a shrill protest like the trumpeting of a bull elephant, and the nails began to pull out of the ironlike chestnut beams. With one debonair twist of the bar, he freed a fine silver board. It parted company with the barn, balanced on end for a split second, then fell silently into the broom grass beside the barn.

"There's a good oak board for your picture frames," said Harley. "Twenty-one inches wide if it's an inch."

"Looks more like chestnut to me," I said.

Harley climbed down from his perch, lifted the board with his toe, and kicked it over in the grass.

"Seasoned chestnut always looks like oak," he said. "Not many folks can tell the difference. But fresh oak is crisper and the saw marks are always sharper." He pointed to a corrugated pattern in the board. "See here?"

Every groove was a signature of one downstroke of some long-gone, water-wheel-operated saw blade. On every upstroke, a cog had pushed the log an eighth of an inch ahead, leaving a corduroy effect of ridges.

"When you see saw-cut marks that crisp," Harley continued, "you can be pretty sure the wood is oak. Looks like it was a big saw blade, too, like the one that was used to mill timber down at New Preston brook. Remember it as a boy. It was there, rusting in the sand, near where we swam, and we used to bang on it at night to make noises like a bell."

"You're quite a detective, Harley," I said, "but I never heard of oak siding on a barn."

He kicked the wood over again and inspected it. "Oh, they had it now and again, but this was a replacement board. Was a floorin' board from the 1700's before it ever reached the barn, though. Second-story floor board, I see. Someone probably put it in to replace a busted pine sidin' board."

"How the devil do you know all that? You're sure guessing a lot!"

Harley showed signs of annoyance at having been doubted. It's not easy for me to recognize annoyance in the average New Englander; it's something you usually have to sense rather than see. I feel that most New Englanders wear a constant look of annoyance. When Harley pushed his hat back on his head with his thumb and sighed at the same time, however, I knew he was annoyed.

"It's floor boardin' all right," he began, "because those holes show where there were plancher nails in them once—those clasp-headed nails they used to make for holding floorboards down. Kept them from popping up. Then there's some lath marks where there was plaster on the underside for a room below; that sure shows it was a second-story floor board, doesn't it? If you look close, you'll see that the lathin' was the kind that's split and opened up like an accordion. They only did that in the 1700's."

Harley was right. An early wooden building usually has more to tell than the average eye sees. And once seen, it is the closest thing to communion with those anonymous pioneers who lived when the American spirit was in its kindling stage. The nails and screws used, the door panels and latches, the laths and the moldings, the way a structure is put together—all these things tend to date any house. The nail holes, the worn stairs and floorings, additions and eliminations made as the years went by,

24

Dating an old building.....

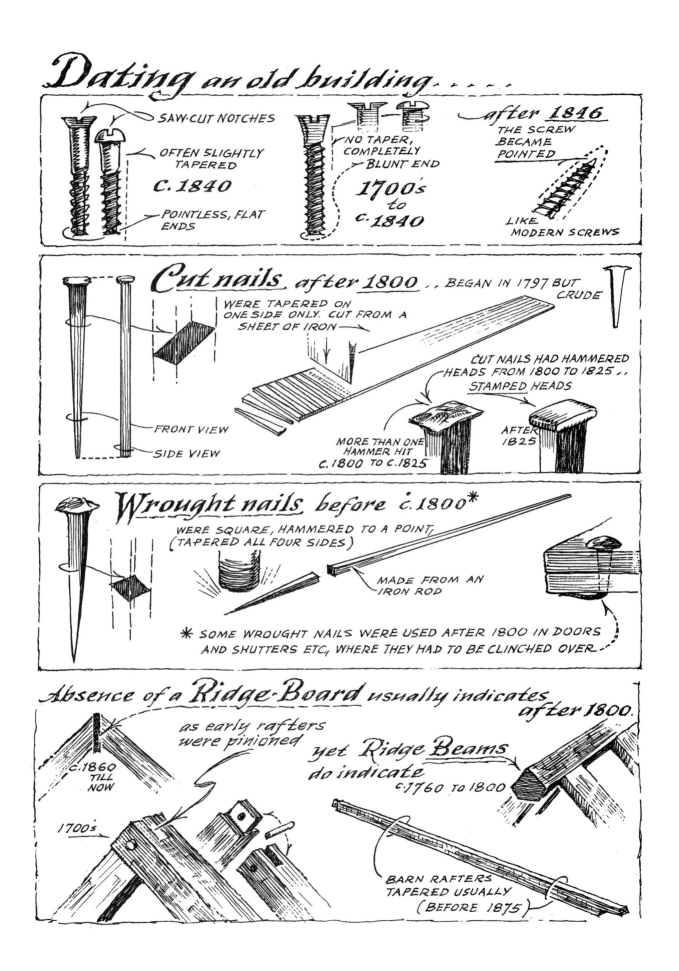

SAW-CUT NOTCHES

OFTEN SLIGHTLY TAPERED
C.1840

POINTLESS, FLAT ENDS

NO TAPER, COMPLETELY BLUNT END
1700's to C.1840

after 1846
THE SCREW BECAME POINTED

LIKE MODERN SCREWS

Cut nails after 1800 .. BEGAN IN 1797 BUT CRUDE

WERE TAPERED ON ONE SIDE ONLY. CUT FROM A SHEET OF IRON

CUT NAILS HAD HAMMERED HEADS FROM 1800 TO 1825 .. STAMPED HEADS

FRONT VIEW

SIDE VIEW

MORE THAN ONE HAMMER HIT C.1800 TO C.1825

AFTER 1825

Wrought nails before c.1800*

WERE SQUARE, HAMMERED TO A POINT, (TAPERED ALL FOUR SIDES)

MADE FROM AN IRON ROD

* SOME WROUGHT NAILS WERE USED AFTER 1800 IN DOORS AND SHUTTERS ETC, WHERE THEY HAD TO BE CLINCHED OVER.

Absence of a Ridge-Board usually indicates after 1800.

as early rafters were pinioned

yet Ridge Beams do indicate c.1760 To 1800

C.1860 TILL NOW

1700's

BARN RAFTERS TAPERED USUALLY (BEFORE 1875)

Plastering Laths leave dark marks on old beams.

STRAIGHT, CLEAN,
UNIFORM MARKS,
INDICATE
Sawed laths
(AFTER C. 1850)

(LOOK FOR SQUARE NAIL
HOLES FOR EARLY
LATH MARKS)

rare
*Accordian
Riven
Laths*
c. 1730
to
c. 1830

old
*Riven
Laths*
1700's
to
c. 1820
IRREGULAR, ROUGH MARKS

Saw marks indicate date too.

1700's to c. 1860

1600's to 1750's

MORE
MODERN

Circular blades
AFTER 1840, TILL NOW.
WIDE, REGULAR CUTS

Up-and-down mill.
REGULAR, VERTICAL,
CRISP, UNIFORM CUTS

Pit-saw (by hand).
SLANTED, IRREGULAR,
FUZZED, NOT UNIFORM

tell the story of those who lived in it. Most old houses have been so often remodeled, however, that sometimes only the nails and boards and beams of the cellar or the attic can be relied upon to be original.

The antiquarian might argue that his interest in antiques is an appreciation of historic atmosphere, a love of the beauty of pleasing decay. More often, however, his interest in antique art boils down to a reverence for the individuality of the past, what man once stood for, the way he lived and the thoughts he thought.

On my wall I have an early American axe, which is constantly the subject of good-natured joking. A carpenter once said to me, "If you like old tools that much, I'll give you some of my old hammers to hang on your wall." It made a good joke, but it also made me think. His hammer, to me, would be the emblem of a six-hour day, the temporary things we so often build nowadays, and the fact that one modern hammer is just like any other modern hammer. My axe is much more than an ornament with pleasing lines. It is a symbol.

The door from the old barn has become a symbol, too. I saved it and made it into a kitchen-table top. To those who chide me and say they have some good old tables "just the thing to make doors out of," I explain, like a good antiquarian, that I use my barn door as a table just because I like its old wood. But there's much more to it than that. Take those scratches just above where the latch used to be. They indicate almost a century of match-lighting. "It seems odd," I remarked to Harley when we were taking the door down, "that a farmer would light matches on his way into his barn. Barns don't last very long that way."

"That farmer," said Harley, "smoked a pipe. Guess he did just like my dad used to do—never smoked inside the barn, but after the animals were bedded down and the door was locked, *then* he lit his pipe. Those scratches, I'd say, were made on the way out."

I recall that when I was researching the old phrase about "knocking on wood," I learned that the New England farmer used to knock on his barn door "for luck" after closing it up for the night. Perhaps my door, too, has been knocked with thousands of such prayers. I like to think so.

Formerly, when I breakfasted alone, I would read the advertisements on the cornflakes box. Now I look at the scratches on my historiographic table and I enjoy musing about the old barn. There are also scratches below, where the door handle used to be, made by a large dog. I guess the farmer had a little dog, too, for there are scratches lower down. Once I thought they might have been from the same dog, first when he was young and then when he was big; but that wouldn't account for his growing-up time.

Then there's a half-round hole where a mouse used to make his own exit and entrance, and another where a mouse began to gnaw his way through, and then for some reason left off. A melancholy thought. It reminds me of a verse from an old country song:

There's an old mouse chewin' on my pantry door,
He must have chewed for a month or more.
When he gets through he'll sure be sore
Fer there ain't a durn thing in there!

Right in the middle of my door-table is the mark of a big square hand-wrought nail where something must have hung, and I like to think it was a Christmas wreath. I recall a mantel in my house where there were some hundred nail holes from Christmas stockings which had been hung there. There were small square holes from eighteenth-century hand-wrought tacks, then the marks of nineteenth-century cut-tacks, and finally the round holes from more recent Christmases.

Actually most early farmers put wreaths not on their house doors, but on their barn doors, because the barn was more symbolic of that holy night. According to an old legend, on Christmas Eve the farm animals are supposed to speak to one another. There is something of Christmas about a barn and its manger.

When I first moved to the village of Warren, I was asked to judge the Christmas decorations on the houses. After touring miles of roads lined with houses decorated by plastic Santas that flashed on and off, and even one neon-lighted Virgin Mary, we came upon a place that truly breathed the spirit of the first Noël. It was a long, dimly lit structure, completely void of cheap ornaments, nestling into a snowy hillside with an almost holy dignity. "That's it!" I said. "First prize!"

"My lands," said my guide, "that isn't anyone's home—that's just an old chicken house."

But it still deserved the prize.

Maybe the nail hole in my door-table wasn't for a wreath. Maybe it was for a "For Sale" sign or even a sheriff's notice, but I enjoy musing over worn old wood and trying to decipher the story it so often has to tell. When Harley eats from my barn door, he seldom neglects to tell me about the new formica table that he got with trading stamps. I know he is obliquely criticizing the holes and marks in my poor table.

Although most early American houses were completely influenced by

The Chicken House

Old World architecture, during the 1700's there evolved a series of door designs that might be considered true Americana. The two-board batten door and the same door with continuous battens (lined or double-door) were beautiful in their simplicity and as strong as the virgin American wood from which they were made. Often a door would be made from a single board, and I found one (dated 1742) with a width of thirty-two inches.

In the pioneer days, doors were often symbols. Just as girls filled hope chests, young men planned doors for the houses they would someday build. A house might be built of local pine and chestnut, but the door was considered something special and the wood was often sassafras panels, apple or cherry, or even mahogany brought from the West Indies or Central America. A godly man might prefer a Christian door with stiles (vertical pieces) and rails (horizontal pieces) that formed a Christian cross. A superstitious person might put a Maltese cross in the lower section and thereby make a "witch door" to keep out the evil spirits, or frame the door with ash to make the spell more potent.* Sometimes the inner surface of a door matched the paneling or wainscoting of the room.

* *The ash tree was thought to have special magic to ward off sickness and evil spirits. No snake (so the legend goes) would cross a barrier of ash leaves.*

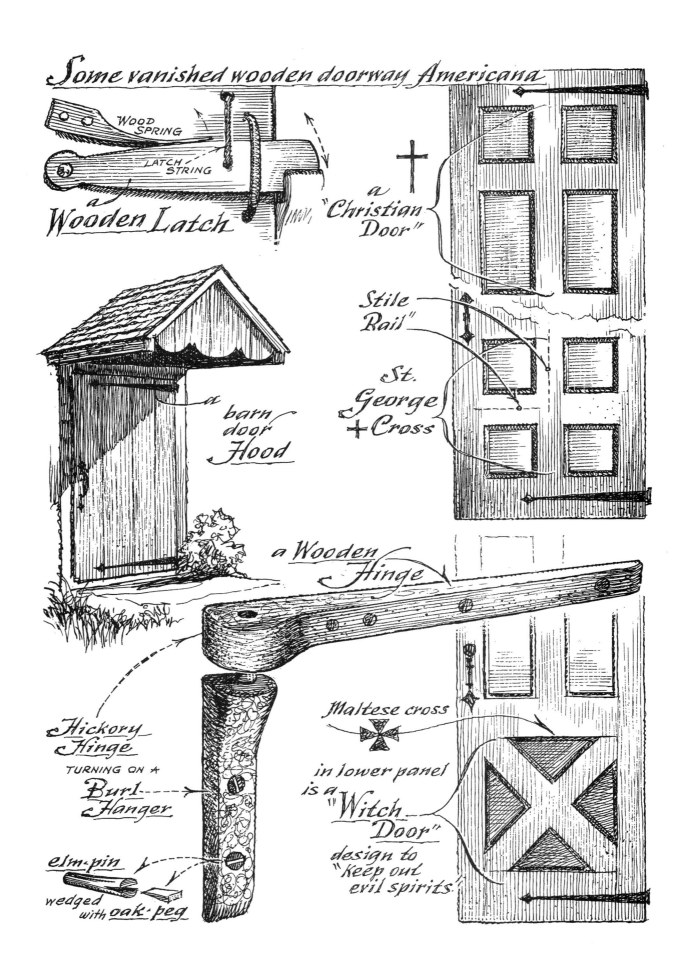

Some vanished wooden doorway Americana

WOOD SPRING

LATCH STRING

a Wooden Latch

a "Christian Door"

Stile Rail"

St. George Cross

a barn door Hood

a Wooden Hinge

Hickory Hinge
TURNING ON A
Burl Hanger

elm-pin
wedged with oak-peg

Maltese cross

in lower panel is a "Witch Door"

design to "keep out evil spirits"

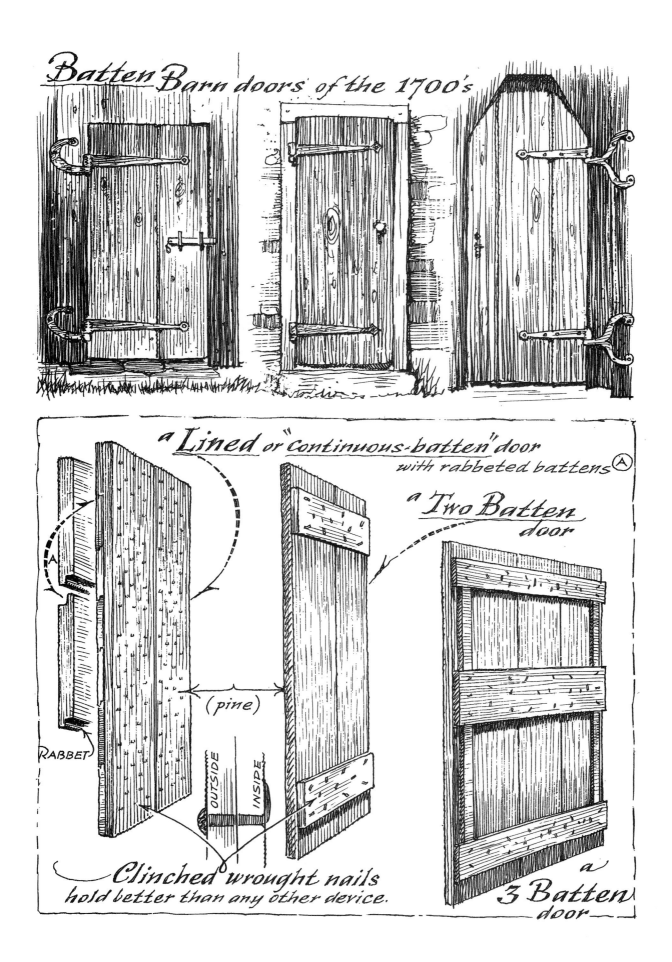

Batten Barn doors of the 1700's

a "Lined or "Continuous-batten" door
with rabbeted battens Ⓐ

a "Two Batten door

RABBET

(pine)

OUTSIDE INSIDE

Ⓐ

a
3 Batten door

Clinched wrought nails
hold better than any other device.

But whatever the design, it was usually the best example of craftsmanship in the whole house.

The stylish sheathed barn door with wooden hinges, wooden locks, and wooden cross-bar for blocking it at night, the door with a closet for guns (or canes), the door set at a slightly leaning-outward angle (so when it opened, it automatically swung all the way back and stayed there)—these, sadly, have become obsolete Americana. The once popular hood that accompanied most barn doors deserves a revival if only for its protection of the entranceway from the weather.

When I began taking my barn down, the only part that I needed was its covering, those boards to make my frames. But when their removal began to expose big chestnut beams underneath, I felt compelled to find some use for them also. Some of the beams had long cracks in them, and I wondered how much this had weakened them.

"Don't worry about it," said Harley. "If it's a heart shake, the beam is just about as strong as ever."

Heart shake? That one took me a few days to research. But what I came up with was that any natural wood crack is known as a "shake" or "check." I always thought a shake was a rough shingle. It still is, in the southern Appalachians where Elizabethan English persists. There the word "shake" also means "to split." Whereas New Englanders would "rive" their shingles with a froe, down south they would "shake" them. In New England and New York, people call a split in timber a "check," but this only originated from a Dutch mispronunciation of the old word "shake," to split.

I learned, too, that there are several kinds of wood shakes, and I have tried to define them in my drawings. These splits or clefts are started by a too rapid loss of sap during seasoning, which causes an unequal contraction between the inner and outer part of the piece of wood. Harley's theory had some truth in it, for the lengthwise splits known as "heart shakes" are not so weakening as the curved slashes that wander, corkscrewlike, around a beam.

Knots are far more weakening than shakes, and when knots appeared on the lower side of a ceiling beam, the old-timers used to slice them out

Sheathed Barn Doors of the 1700's,
(locked from the insides).

Bead

Pennsylvania
Lancaster County   Berks County

Ship-lap

New York
State Dutch

"Shakes" or "Checks" in timber

Season Check · **Heart Check** · **Star Check** · **Ring Check** · **Cup Check**

Logs seasoned "in the round" tend to split open from circular contraction
(much exaggerated)

King post joint

how a check can weaken a wooden joint,

and how

a _KNOT_ can weaken the tensile (stretched) stress portion of a beam.

Knot in area of Compression is not weakening but this one is

...so is this one

vertical knot

with an axe on the theory that the loss of wood there would be less weakening than the knot. Often when an old house is being remodeled and the ceiling beams are exposed, these indentations cause some disappointment, for they are usually taken as an indication that some earlier remodeling had been done. Knots on the sides or upper parts of the beams were compressive, and therefore not weakening, so they were never cut out.

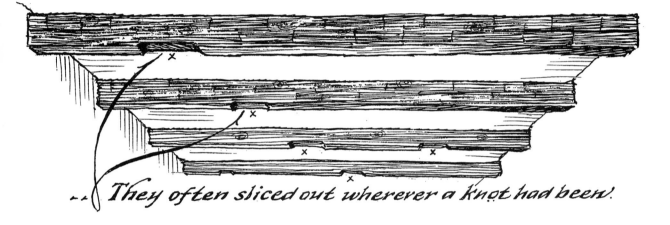

They often sliced out wherever a knot had been.

Builders today wouldn't think of using a ten-inch square beam for framing a small house; in fact, lumber yards don't carry that kind of wood. But the early builder used animal anatomy as his model and he thought of framework as being the bones of his house and the sheathing or clapboards as being its outer skin. Today's house has bones only as strong as its skin. At one time a house's bones were big and much stronger than necessary, but they really furnished the weight to keep the house from blowing away. I have slept in an old barn when a gale was blowing and there was some peculiar comfort and sense of solidity in being aware of the tons of oak and chestnut that made up the framing.

I have heard complaints about the creaking of big house timbers during changes in the weather, but that is something soon accepted by the woodwise. It is as natural a phenomenon as the swaying of a bridge or skyscraper in the wind, and it is something for which a good designer actually allows. To permit this movement, big timbers were pinned with

Ways of making a wooden pin stay put. (1700's)

Square peg for a round hole

FOR A TIGHT WEDGE

nicked pin ANCHORS ITSELF IN

the "OFFSET PIN"

OFFSET

THIS HOLE LOWER THAN THIS ONE

SO THAT THE PEG WEDGES THE BRACE MORE TIGHTLY

a rare peg was **larger than the hole!**
(OFTEN USED IN CHAIR-RAILS)

Hammered while green, it stayed put tightly

Sometimes pegs were pegged to stay put

...and pins were pinned in place

SOMETIMES FOUND IN MILL BEAMS

...and sometimes the pin didn't lock the beams together at all, but locked a wedge in place

c.1760

wood instead of being fastened with iron. The old trunnels (treenails) allowed joints to move with atmospheric changes without being torn apart. Just as the bark on trees tightens when a cold air mass passes through the forest, the great timbers in early structures move on their joints and sometimes make resounding booms through the night.

Early fastening pins or trunnels were just hand-cut pegs, but during the middle 1700's framers used interesting methods for making them secure. Sometimes they were nicked to keep them from working their way out; often the hole in one of the two connecting beams was slightly offset so the trunnel would have to be wedged in tightly. Some framers hammered a square pin of green wood into a round hole. Some didn't pin the beams together at all, but pinned a wedge instead (which left the end of the beam unweakened by any hole).

Pins were usually cut on a shaving horse with a drawknife, but by the 1800's, when many bridges were being built and there was a need for more and larger fasteners, pins were cut on lathes and manufactured by the thousands. They could be ordered by the barrel, and they were sent to the buyer soaked in linseed oil.

It is amazing how often old trunnels become wedded to the joint (it is as if they had been welded there). In disconnecting the rafters of my barn, it was almost impossible to hammer the peak trunnels out. But it was while trying to do so that I came upon something interesting: near the peak of one end-rafter were the remains of what Harley called a

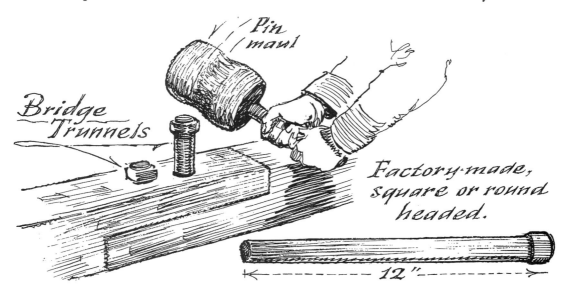

Pin
maul

Bridge
Trunnels

Factory-made,
square or round
headed.

←-------- 12" --------→

"wetting bush," a small sapling that had been nailed there upright by the builder (as is still the custom) when the roof framing was finished.

I knew what Harley meant, for I had encountered the phrase before. The carpenters of a house I once had built asked my wife to please be present the next day when the workmen "wet the bush." Ruth could hardly wait till I returned to ask me what they meant. It took some searching of my memory and some imagination before I realized that they referred to the old New England custom of putting a sapling atop a new house and drinking a toast as a sort of christening ceremony. I am sure they didn't know where it came from, but the phrase "wetting the bush" is as old as the Druids.

Finding the remains of that ceremonial sapling, still held in place by the hand-forged nails, made me all the more reluctant to take the old barn down. The "bush" had certainly brought luck to the building—for about two centuries.

By now, Harley knew my interest in all things made of wood. He didn't ask me if I wanted to keep this or that wooden object, but simply put them in a pile where I might examine them. And before long I had a small collection of harness hooks made from the crotches of tree limbs.

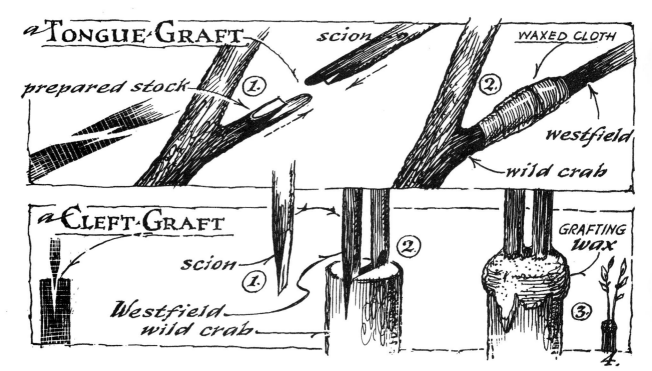

38

a
Neck yoke

the strong, convenient
Tree Crotch

Bucket Hooks

for maple sap,
water, milk
etc.

a
shelf
bracket

a Harness
hook

Designed to hold weight.

"The wood in a tree crotch," Harley explained, "seasons like iron. It makes a good hook. Those harness hooks are all apple crotches. You can still smell the fruitwood if you rub it."

"I thought they seldom cut down good apple trees in the old days."

"You're right, they didn't. But like as not those harness hooks were made from apple prunings. About this time of year my father used to take me up on that hill yonder with a load of Westfield prunings* to graft onto wild crabs."

"Wild crabs?"

Harley sighed at my ignorance. "Crabs are just wild apple trees. They don't bear fruit worth a hang, but they're strong. An orchard seedling wouldn't last through a New England winter, but a forest crab will stand up to weather like any strong tree. We used to tongue-graft and

* Some country people call a scion for grafting a "pruning."

39

1865   1965

cleft-graft Westfields onto the wild crabs. Now the whole mountain has good apples."

I confessed I'd never heard of "Westfields" either, but then there are a great many things I've never heard of.

Harley continued, "The old folks called them Seek-no-furthers. Never did know why."

"Sounds like something they made up themselves," I said.

"No, it's an old English name. Fellow from Westfield, Massachusetts, is supposed to have planted the first one on top of Dudleytown Mountain back in the 1700's. I saw it about fifty years ago and they say it's still there."

"I know that apple trees can last for a hundred years, but I didn't think they could live for two centuries."

"Oh, in a way it's not the same tree," said Harley. "It just kept growing and falling down and growing up again. Some day I'll look for it. If it's still there, I'll show it to you."

That night I thought about Harley's story of the Seek-no-further apple tree that "kept falling and growing up again." It seemed more interesting than working on the barn. And so before noon of the next

40

day, we were shoulder-deep in thickets of a forest slope searching for the old tree.

"There she is!" Harley said suddenly. "She's done it again! That's the old tree I carved my initials on when I was about ten years old."

He sliced away some forest brush so I could get a better look. Resting on a bed of leaves and young shoots was the hulk of an old apple tree well over three feet in diameter. It had fallen from old age, yet some of the branches which were still living when the old tree fell had struck into the ground and miraculously taken root to become offspring of the parent tree. As the fallen trunk decayed, new apple saplings had rooted all around it, giving the appearance of a family gathered around a dead giant on his bier. The old tree had dug its branches like fingers into the earth, a strange and striking sequence of resurrection.

This process had perhaps occurred over and over, each fallen tree plunging downslope. The hulk we now beheld was probably about sixty feet from the original tree. I traced the path of resurrections uphill to a piling of stones such as might have been grouped along a rail fence. Here, I thought, the first Seek-no-further apple tree might have grown. I wondered what the countryside had looked like then.

... there I imagined grew the first "Seek-no-further" apple tree.

1865

The heft and feel of a well-worn handle,
The sight of shavings that curl from a blade;
The logs in the woodpile, the sentiment of huge
                   beams in an old-fashioned house;
The smell of fresh cut timber and the pungent
                   fragrance of burning leaves;
The crackle of kindling and the hiss of burning logs.
Abundant to all the needs of man, how poor the world
                   would be
Without wood.

Everard Hinrichs

The Cleared Land

Until the 1860's the farmer was hailed as the most noble and independent man in American society, but suddenly he became a national comic figure named Reuben or Silas, with funny boots, chin whiskers, and hayseeds in his ears. He and his ways were old-fashioned, and "old-fashioned" had become a shameful word. *The Country Gentleman* of 1865 ran a column called, "Why Do Young Men Leave the Farm?" When the boys came home from the war, it was usually just to pick up their clothes and head for a job in the city.

During the period of the Civil War, the upheaval of American society resulted in much ugliness and some deterioration of taste. Before that time, agriculture and the preservation of tradition were a cherished part of the good life, but from then on the philosophy of "change for the sake of change" became a dominant force in American thinking.

Hardly were the battles over when the iron factories, which had been making the hardware of war, began seeking inventors and inviting them to set their sights on peacetime production. For a while there were born countless intricate machines devised to do any job faster and poorer. By

1865 there were four hundred and fifty-two all-metal apple-parers invented, yet the old-timers preferred the paring knife. William Morris recognized his age, remarking that the great achievement of those post-bellum days was "the making of machines which were the wonders of invention, skill, and patience, used for the production of measureless quantities of worthless makeshifts."

Anything which hitherto had been made of wood was quickly duplicated and mass-produced in iron. And to replace the beauty of handmade design, ornaments were added. A locomotive stack might be fluted and flowered; a steam engine's walking-beam might become a replica of an Ionic column. Carpenter's tools, house architecture, and even farm machinery got the treatment. It was an era of doodads and decoration. The American reverence for wood had become old-fashioned and obsolete almost overnight, and the individual makers of wooden things became rare artisans.

There rose a quest for new ways to use wood, even to the point of wasting it. The corduroy roads of the past (where logs had been laid out in wet places) were revived in the form of sawed planks, and plans were made for all main highways to be "plankroads." Even the city streets used wooden blocks. Sawmills became so busy and so wasteful that navigation was often stopped by the sawdust and chips which were emptied into the rivers. Often such blockage had to be burned, and "river fires" that burned for weeks added hazard to blockage. One average-size sawmill at Orono, Maine, was required by fire-prevention law to burn 36 thousand cords of scrap wood a year.

The English criticized us, saying that the Americans "seem to hate trees and cannot wait to cut them down." Indeed, we seemed to have gone out of our way to use wood, solely because it was so plentiful. British locomotives were designed to run on coke in the 1850's, while the American railroads were using hardwood fuel.*

* In 1865 the amount of wood used for fuel in America was possibly at its height. Steamboats and locomotives were still using wood, and it is difficult to estimate the amount used yearly. But the Boston and Worcester Railroad used 8,000 cords and the Western Railroad (between Worcester and Albany) used 18,000 cords. All of the railroads in Massachusetts used 53,710 cords. The wood by this time was mainly pine, and the price per cord averaged $3.25.

46

a log jam in a "river of wood". c. 1865

Looking north from Cornwall over Connecticut's Berkshires, one sees an unending series of rolling hills. From the Revolution to the Civil War this land had given most of its tree growth to feed the iron furnaces. Every thirty-five years, which is sufficient time for hardwood trees to grow into useful timber, the hills were harvested. In the Berkshires, people called it being "coaled." The furnaces there were making about three million dollars' worth of iron each year and over half of that was paid for wood consumed as iron-making charcoal. But money value of those days is a poor basis for comparing quantity now, so instead try to imagine a square of forest four miles long on each boundary. That much had to be stripped for one year's production of Berkshire iron. "Stripped" is no exaggeration, for should you have happened to view that countryside from any elevated point, you could have counted the big trees on the fingers of your hands. The big trees appeared two at a time, placed as "husband and wife trees" when a house was built. They were usually on

47

"Husband-and-wife trees."

the east side of the house or at each side of the entrance; you could pick out the farmhouses on any New England landscape by these double clumps of green.

Hidden in the ravines and river valleys, however, there were still groves of tall virgin pine. They stretched skyward above the sea of forest shade in their effort to reach sunlight, their trunks mastlike before they burst into foliage, often as high as seventy-five feet. Some still bore the scars of the "King's Broad Arrow" that had marked them a century before as property of the British Navy. They were left standing only because charcoal made from them was unsuitable for the making of iron. The pitch in pine could explode into flame and destroy a week's work of charcoal making. So the "cathedrals," as people used to call pine groves, continued to flourish while the surrounding hills were being coaled off.

Pine charcoal was considered by some people to be a superior grade for a few special uses (indeed the United States mint in Philadelphia used it), but the iron makers insisted on hardwood charcoal. When you realize what specialists early Americans were and how knowledgeable they were in the characteristics of each kind of wood, it is understandable that pine should be considered inferior as charcoal. (A chair might contain fifteen kinds of wood, each serving a specific purpose, one wood often reacting against another to keep the joints tight. Even a fishing rod of three pieces was made of different woods—ash for the first joint, hickory for the second, and bamboo for the tip.)

48

Pine wood was used for kindling: except in an emergency, few would consider using it as fuel. It burned too quickly, it scattered sparks, and it made a very hard and inflammable kind of chimney soot. Even its ashes, which ordinarily would be used for making soap, were inferior to those of hardwoods.

Wood needed to throw out a given amount of heat.

Hickory   *White Oak*   *Hard Maple*   *Soft Maple*   *White Pine*

The early pitch pine of New England was called candlewood, and it was actually sold for that purpose, particularly for lighting one's way from the house to outbuildings or for carrying a flame from one fireplace to another. Even now when you find a bundle of candlewood tucked away in some attic or over an ancient barn beam, there will be enough pitch in the slivers to make them ignite at the touch of a lighted match. Yet pine's softwood classification kept it out of the early American woodpile.

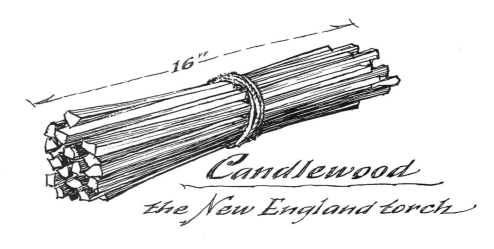

16"

Candlewood
the New England torch

49

It was in the late 1800's that the American farmer lost his special regard for wood as a fuel, even to the extent of forsaking the many pleasures of the hearth. By 1900 the farm fireplace had been walled up and the kitchen stove had taken its place. Wood was still burned, but it was shoved into the stove without ceremony; though you face a fireplace and enjoy the flames, when you shut the fire up in a black iron box, you tend to turn your back on it. It is strange that most of the walled-up fireplaces still contain their andirons—perhaps because they, too, were unwanted symbols of the obsolete and old-fashioned.*

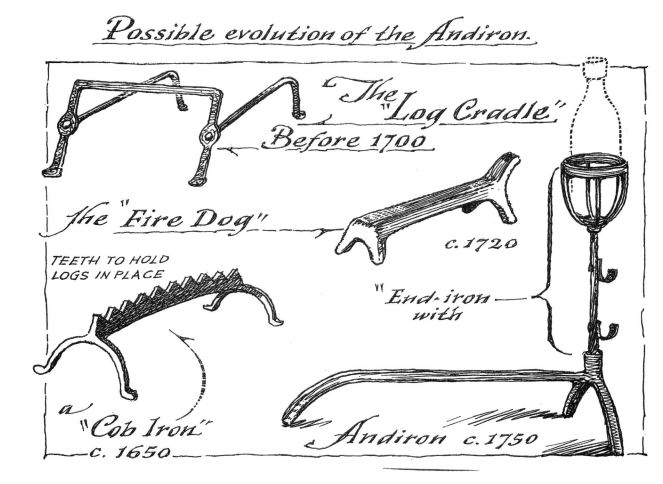

Possible evolution of the Andiron.

The "Log Cradle" Before 1700

The "Fire Dog"

c.1720

TEETH TO HOLD LOGS IN PLACE

"End-iron with

a "Cob Iron" c. 1650

Andiron c.1750

* *Andirons were really a British device, never a product of early American design, for the colonists of the 1600's made simple "fire dogs" for holding logs, using a "lug-pole" (a heavy green stick) for holding pots by a chain. In the 1700's, when spits became popular, end-irons were added to the fire dogs for holding the spits.*

The farm woodlot began to disappear by the late 1800's. At one time it was the farmer's main cash crop; his corn and grain and vegetables were mostly for his own family's use, but spending money came from the wood for splints, barrel hoops, shingles, charcoal and the countless other things that were harvested from woodlots. By 1865 most cultivated hardwood groves were gone, and in the Berkshires as far as the eye could see, there was only a rolling patchwork of farm plots held together with a thin black stitching of stone fences. Even as stone fences grew, the wood rails that usually lay on top of them were being sold to the charcoal-makers; the man whose land was enclosed with whole timber was considered well-off indeed. In the South, where stones were less abundant, there were farmers who had abandoned their land and buildings for no other reason than a lack of new fence material.

In Connecticut, when snake-rail fences began to rot and no fresh replacements were available, farmers piled stones around to keep them upright, so that in time there grew a sort of "snake-stone" formation. Years later when the rails disintegrated and disappeared and new forest growth came, a riddle arose. Why should anyone choose to build a zig-zag stone fence? And without realizing that the forest was once cleared fields, there are those today who wonder at stone fences built directly through dense woods.

Most history books comment upon wire fencing as comparatively recent Americana, giving such dates as 1873 for the invention of barbed wire and 1883 for woven wire. Yet Benjamin Franklin is said to have experimented with wire for enclosing cattle, and a lengthy "Account of Wire Fencing" was read at the Philadelphia Agricultural Society on January 2, 1816. By then, there were several Pennsylvania farms using wire fences.

The 1816 account spoke of "living trees connected with rails of wire," and true to the early American philosophy of looking far ahead, it compared the cost of wire fencing with wood fencing over a period of fifty years. It came to the conclusion that there was a cash saving of $1,329 per hundred acres enclosed. The plan, however, was indeed unique for it enabled the fence to *earn money!* Why plant dead posts in

Fence through rocky field

The explanation of Zig-Zag stone fences through New England forests.

1. (1700's)..

Field cleared of rocks, piled around fence.

2. (1800's)..

3.

..the snake rail fence has rotted away and left the clearing stones to be seen now

... winding through woodlands.

the ground and wait for them to rot? Why not plant live trees instead and let them bear fruit and nuts and firewood which would then give profit to the farmer? Using a hundred acres as an example, the Society suggested the following plan of live tree posts and showed what they might earn a farmer within fifty years (allowing no harvest for the first ten years of growth):

52

244	apple trees producing	$1 per year	....	$ 244
30	cherry trees "	50¢ per year	....	15
20	pear trees "	50¢ per year	....	10
10	plum trees "		....	3
10	shellbark trees "		....	10
50	chestnut trees "		....	12
5	butternut trees "		....	20
5	English walnuts "		....	5
20	walnut trees "		....	5
250	buttonwood trees (24 cords firewood taken from tops)		....	72
				$ 396

multiplied by 40 years' harvests $15,840
deduct the cost of wire rails 1,751
to the credit of live tree posts and wire fence in 50 years $14,089

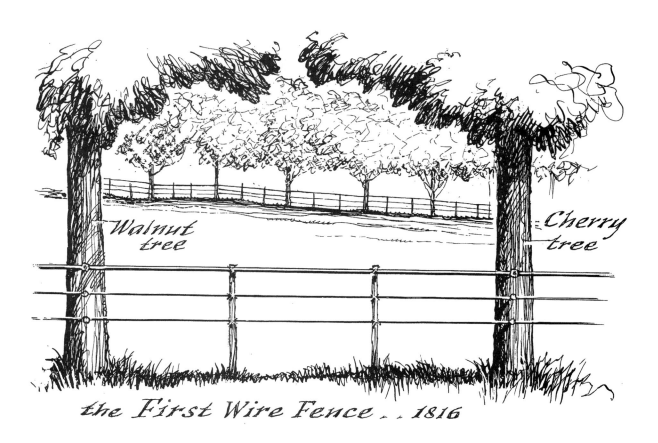

Walnut tree

Cherry tree

the First Wire Fence .. 1816

"Besides this great earning," the account goes on, "the soil around the fence will benefit by shade and the falling of leaves and twigs. Whoever might wish to see a wire fence of this plan may observe its benefits at R. Watkin's Tavern, at the Falls of Schuylkill." The report is signed, "Hon. Richard Peters, pres. of Agrict. Society, January the second, 1816."

But America was a country of wooden wealth, and wire fences seemed sacrilegious to the average farmer; it took another century for the wire fence to become generally popular, and then only because there was no wood left for making wooden fences.

After the Civil War, the U.S. Army made inventory of the nation's seven million miles of wood fences, because they were considered to be of importance in the field of battle. This might sound strange, yet the word *fence* was originally short for *defense*, and the use of a fence to hold in cattle was something quite American and recent. General James Brisbin, who took over the job, estimated there was "over two *billion* [a word seldom used in those days] dollars worth of wood fencing in America," and the cost of repairing it came to about one hundred million dollars a year. At the then current average of three hundred dollars a mile, our wood fences had added up to something like the national debt.

It can be understood why farmers were very particular in their choice of fencing material. To replace a rotted fence around a five hundred acre farm might be a full year's work. If locust, cedar, chestnut, walnut, or white oak (fencing was chosen in that order) was not available nearby, a man might haul proper fencing by ox-cart from a considerable distance. So it was that Jeremy Wolcott contemplated such a journey. His land at Cornwall had been fenced with oak some twenty years before by his father, and the town fence-viewer expressed wonderment at oak lasting that long. Some of it was too far gone for selling to the charcoal man even as scrap.

"The idea of journeying to New Haven and back with loads of wood," said Jeremy's wife, "sounds ridiculous to me. Hauling chestnut rails to sell is bad enough, but hauling back locust posts that you've bought . . . that seems like such a waste of time. Besides, I'll miss you."

"Jonathan will take good care of you, Sarah, and it will take his mind

54

from all the war he's seen. There's nothing like splitting rails to rest a man's mind and give him healthful exercise. By the time I've returned he'll have enough new rails split to start the new fence."

"Won't they have to season?"

"Chestnut rails can season right in the fence if we hang them right. It's the posts that must be seasoned. The Long Island posts have been seasoned for two years; with a little charring they should last as long as we do. Connecticut needs posts as much as Long Island needs rails."

"It sounds like 'The Boston Post Riders' to me," said Sarah.

"The Boston Post Riders" was a well-known story of early times, for when the road was opened, two mail riders started out from opposite ends, riding at full tilt to save time. They met midway, exchanged sacks, and sped back to their respective towns. It seemed like a timesaver until a small boy asked, "Why don't you just pass each other and keep going? You're not saving any time."

"Well, it may sound like 'The Boston Post Riders' to you," said Jeremy, "but it makes sense to me."

The story of Long Island's locust trees is of historic interest. The scraggly locust that looks like a dying tree even at its best, during the summer, is perhaps the only remaining sign of early Long Island farm days. Native to North America, the locust was brought from the Appalachians to Great Britain in the middle 1600's. There it was rejected as wood that splits easily, warps badly, and works with much difficulty. The English, however, adopted it as hedge or fence material because of its thorns. But by the time of the Revolution, after some of the hedges had been left to grow into trees, it was found that full-grown locust trees harbor borers and other insects and "that damned American locust tree" was blamed for all sorts of plagues and banned. Oddly enough at the same time, America was blaming English barberry for a plague of wheat rust, accusing the British of planting barberry wild in order to ruin our wheat crops. A law was passed that barberry could be destroyed even if it meant trespassing to do so.

But Long Island had learned much about locust from the British and began planting it first as low hedging and then left it to grow as fence-

Black Locust . . (common or yellow locust)

LEAVES PODS

Long Island Americana

post material. So well did Long Island become known for its locust trees that it soon suffered a shortage of all other timber. For a while Long Island was "swapping wood," with a regular shipping lane across Long Island Sound, locust going to the Connecticut shore, chestnut and pine coming back to the Island.

The honey locust, so called because its pods contain over twenty-five percent sugar, became an important cattle food on Long Island. Some farmers crushed the pods into a sweet meal and used that instead of sugar in their cooking. But during the timber shortage of the late 1800's, the Island's supply of locust ran out and only those locusts used as hedging or fencing remained. Now one may still see some of these, dying in their old age, fifty feet higher than the hedge of which they once were part, solitary symbols of an era.

Jeremy Wolcott did haul his rails to the shore, and his son did remain behind to get the last of the chestnut (lest the charcoal men got there first). The charcoal burners always were a strange breed, living a lonely

56

life in the forest, almost like wild beasts. And when hardwood became scarce (and later when coal was used for the job of making iron) the charcoal makers' life and habits fell into a deplorable decline. Not only shunned, they were often feared.

At its best, the job of making charcoal was not for any normal human being. The time required for charring a small mound varied from one to two weeks, but with mounds of wood thirty feet or more round, a month was average. During all that time, through every kind of weather, the maker of charcoal lived with his mound, sleeping only in dozes for fear a flame might start and explode into a full fire which would demolish the mound. There was no time for washing; there was seldom more shelter than a bark lean-to. And there were so many things to watch for in a "live mound" that the man became almost part of it.

At first lighting, a black smoke poured from holes in the middle of the mound; this was quickly smothered until a blue haze arose. This was kept

Anatomy of a Charcoal Mound

Center stake

LAYER OF green ferns or wet leaves COVERED BY sod

Logs (SHARP ENDS TOWARD STAKE)

USUALLY FROM 25 TO 40 CORDS.

PLANK BASE

twigs

twigs

Each charcoal man had his own method or recipe for building a good mound

alive by constantly smothering any flames with moist charcoal powder. Then there was a "sweating period" when the mound emitted a yellowish smoke; at that point, moist charcoal or mud was quickly applied until the smoke turned gray. Until the heat subsided, the mound never stopped "working" and neither did the man. By the end of each charring, his body had become completely black outside and exhausted inside. Knowing how and when to walk on the mound was an art in itself, and many a man fell through into the furnacelike heat.

Charcoal during the 1800's was used for many things other than making iron. People cleaned their teeth with it. Although the first results may look ghastly, there is actually nothing more beneficial for teeth than charcoal powder. Swallow some of it? Also good; there is nothing better for upset stomach. It even sweetens the breath. If you want to purify water or remove an offensive odor from anything, use charcoal. Sailors used to throw burnt muffins into their water supply when it became stale or smelly; meat packers used to pack their meats in charcoal. Ice was stored in charcoal, gunpowder was made with it; printer's ink, black paint, medicines, even highways were made from it. In 1865 someone dreamed up this idea, thinking that since charcoal is the longest lasting of materials, a road made of it would be very durable. Timber was piled along the middle of the road and burned right there; then the charred material was raked out and tamped down.

It is interesting to note that early iron is better in many ways than modern iron because of the use of charcoal, which is carbon without imperfections. Some of the tools made from Berkshire iron resist rust and hold an edge better than today's Pennsylvania iron, which is made in a furnace fueled by coal.

Country people made their own charcoal in either cross-laid or tepee-arranged wooden sticks. With wet leaves and sod as covering, and a small hole for draft (and for watching the progress of charring), it took three days and nights for a mound to char completely. When finished, the pile of charcoal simply collapsed within the mound; then the sod covering was removed. This was the only coal known in the early days, and it was needed for all blacksmith work. Charcoal was sifted in a spleen sieve; the fine powder and "charcoal-meal" were saved for cleaning teeth or for the

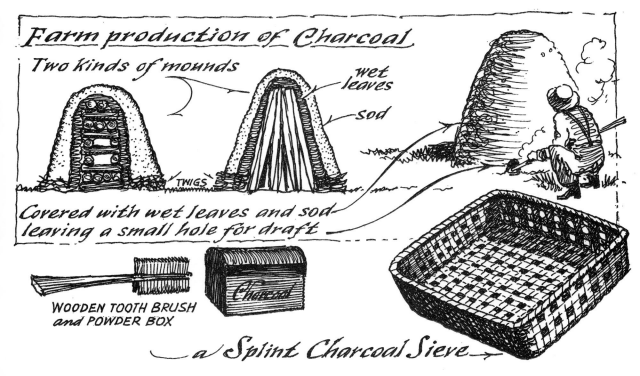

Farm production of Charcoal
Two kinds of mounds
wet leaves
sod
TWIGS
Covered with wet leaves and sod leaving a small hole for draft
WOODEN TOOTH BRUSH and POWDER BOX
Charcoal
— a Splint Charcoal Sieve →

medicine cabinet. In the cities the charcoal vendor sold from his cart at forty cents a barrel (the price at about 1865) and his well-known chant was:

Charcoal by the bushel,
Charcoal by the peck,
Charcoal by the frying pan
Or anyway you lek!

It was an era of charcoal and a time of disappearing trees.

In Cornwall, Connecticut, and wherever iron was made in the Berkshires, you may still see where the burning mounds were: the hardwood is coming back in those hills, except for the chestnut, which reaches about ten feet before it browns and succumbs to the blight of 1904. There are still hulks of chestnut tree trunks stretched across the forest floor or caught in their fall by surrounding limbs. Some are still sound enough to dull the edge of a handsaw. And each spring there are new shoots that rise from stumps cut a century ago by the long-gone charcoal men.

Chestnut . . .

. . . 1904 . . . . still trying to come back

Jonathan Wolcott's work of splitting rails was not made easier by his father's journey to the coast. Ordinarily logs were snaked out of the forest as soon as they were felled, but these logs had been barked and left in place to season, which meant that they had to be split on location in the woodlot. It was the New England custom, for the sake of safety, never to work alone a distance from the house. And the almanac suggested splitting rails later on, during the wane of the moon. Like most people of that time, Jonathan knew that when the almanac spoke of moon phases nothing mystical was intended. It was just a way of identifying time (as our present-day calendars do) by moon positions, and at the same time indicating the periods of the greatest amount of moonlight for jobs that usually continued after darkness. Jonathan had to make use of the waxing Gibbous moon, working until it was almost overhead before he started for home.

Farmers sometimes used bark for tanning hides, but home tanning was difficult and messy work, so most farmers took the hides to town for tanning. Tree bark was either left to rot in the woods or sold to the tanneries. But the Wolcott bark was given to the charcoal men, who in these lean times were glad to have anything that might earn them a dollar.

Jonathan seldom saw them, for they picked up the scraps either early in the morning or late in the evening; the bark would disappear and there would be telltale footprints all about, showing that the Raggies had been there. Perhaps the name Raggy started from the charcoal men who lived around Mount Riga; one seldom knew their names and when one asked, it was often an unpronounceable European name, so they were just called "Rigys" in those days. But when wood became scarce and coal was introduced into iron-making, the Rigys became very poor and ragged. Then the name Raggie seemed to fit even better.

The dull thud of Jonathan's maul could be heard each time he struck the glut to split a log, and the Raggies knew exactly when he started and stopped working. An experienced woodsman could even tell what kind of tree was being worked on and what kind of axe or wedge was being used. The sound of an axe cutting into soft pine is very different

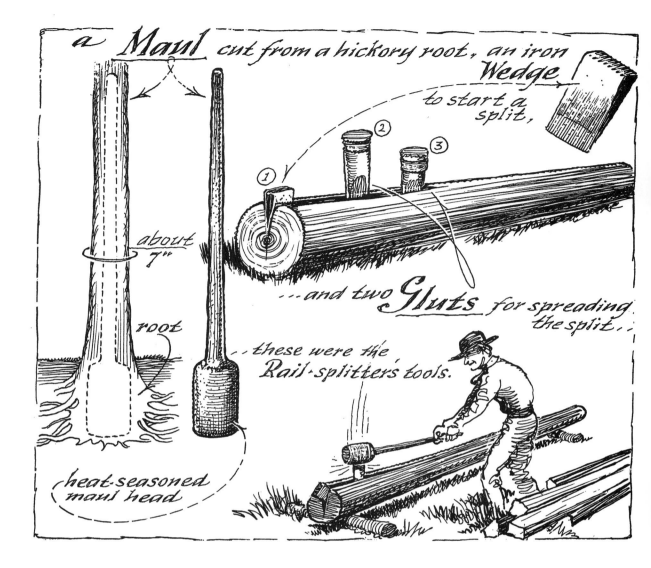

a Maul cut from a hickory root, an iron Wedge to start a split, ...and two Gluts for spreading the split...

about 7"

root

heat-seasoned maul head

these were the Rail-splitter's tools.

from the sharp ping of hardwood being cut; even the sharpness of a blade produces a certain sound to the ear of an expert, and Jonathan had often heard his father say, "Your axe sounds dull, son. Give it a sharpening when you get home."

So one day when Jonathan found some basswood trees in the Wolcott woodlots and felled a few, he was not surprised that the Raggies knew what he was about. The whack of an axe into the softer pulp of linden (or basswood as it was known) had aroused their curiosity. Four Raggies approached him.

62

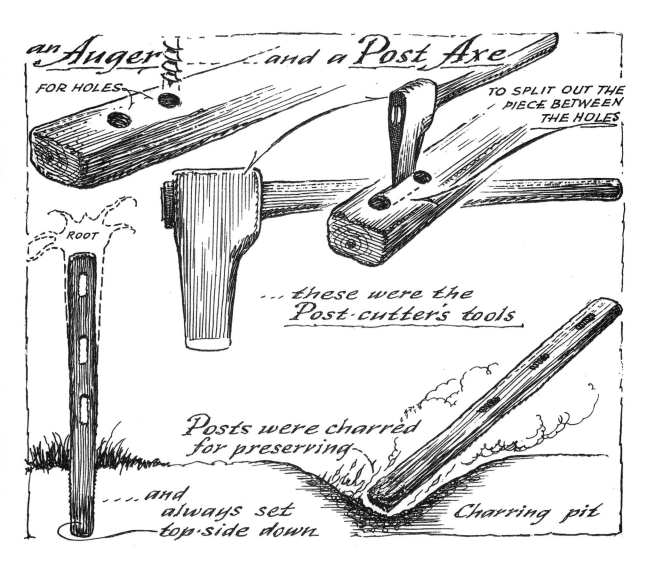

an Auger... ...and a Post Axe

FOR HOLES

TO SPLIT OUT THE
PIECE BETWEEN
THE HOLES

ROOT

...these were the
Post-cutter's tools

Posts were charred
for preserving

...and
always set
top-side down

Charring pit

"Greetings!" said Jonathan, holding a box of snuff in his extended hand.

All four nodded and each took a pinch of snuff, inhaling it in very fine European manner. The American woodsman had learned to wad a pinch of snuff into a ball and place it under his upper lip. These men, thought Jonathan, cannot speak English. But one of them stepped forward and tried his limited vocabulary. He held out a small wooden berry box.

"We need berry-wood for boxes. We will give you berries."

Jonathan knew what he meant. He knew how the Raggies had been

63

living almost exclusively on the berries that grew on the coaled hills. He also knew that the berries could be made into a liquid for which the Raggies had become famous. It was called "rattlesnake medicine," and it helped them to forget bad times. But during the summer they peddled berries in basswood boxes which were made in the nearby village of Milton. They wanted basswood to bring to the box-maker, who would reimburse them for the raw material by giving them a few finished boxes.

Jonathan understood. He held out his hand with five fingers spread.

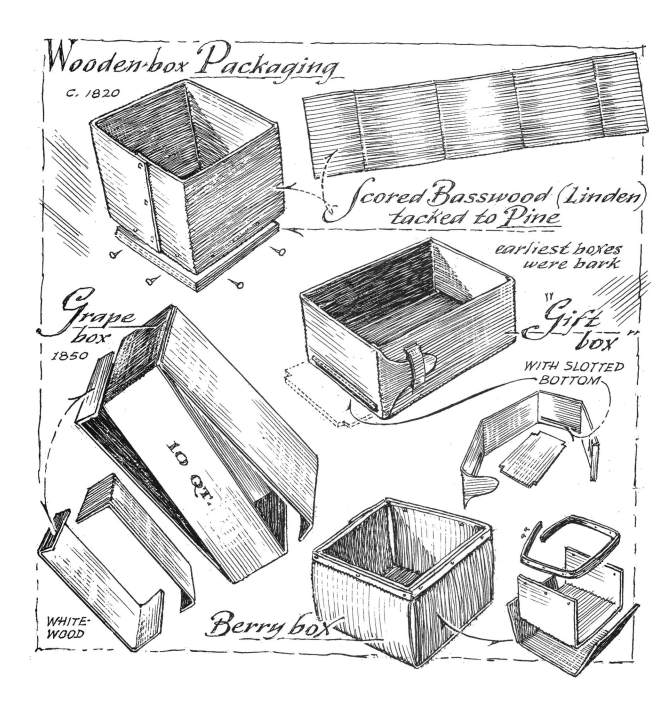

Wooden-box Packaging

C. 1820

Scored Basswood (Linden) tacked to Pine

earliest boxes were bark

"Gift box"

WITH SLOTTED BOTTOM

Grape box 1850

10 QT.

WHITE-WOOD

Berry box

"Five basswood trees," he said. "You take them. No berries. I'm giving you a gift."

With much bowing and many gestures of gratitude, the four men departed.

By the time of the Civil War, boxes were machine-made, and America had started its amazing career of packaging. Paper cartons and paper bags came later, the first patent being for a cone-shaped paper bag in 1867. There are illustrations of Abraham Lincoln waiting on customers with a

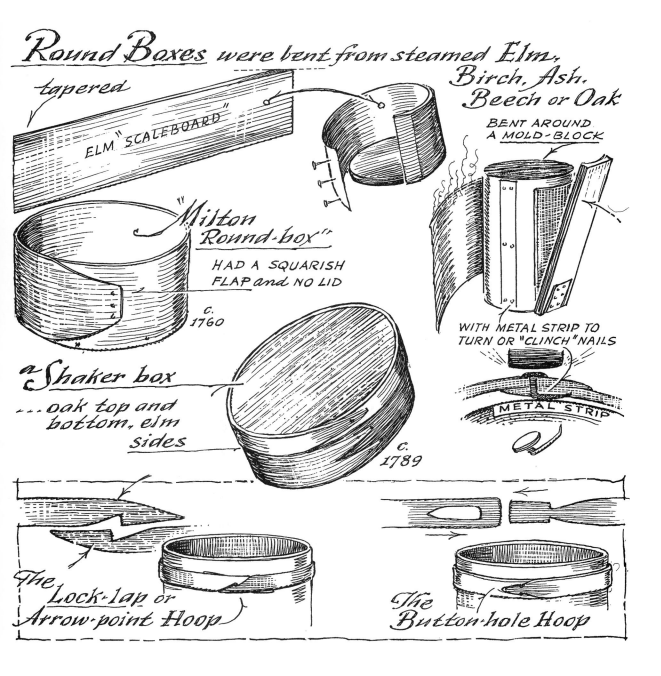

Round Boxes were bent from steamed Elm, Birch, Ash, Beech or Oak

tapered

ELM "SCALEBOARD"

BENT AROUND A MOLD-BLOCK

"Milton Round-box"

HAD A SQUARISH FLAP and NO LID

C. 1760

WITH METAL STRIP TO TURN or "CLINCH" NAILS

METAL STRIP

"Shaker box

...oak top and bottom, elm sides

C. 1789

The Lock-lap or Arrow-point Hoop

The Button-hole Hoop

square type of paper bag, but these really didn't appear until after 1872. Before that, you went to a store with your own basket or jug or cloth bag; the idea of a wooden package designed to be sold along with the food it contained was something uniquely American.

The first wooden boxes were from Maine; they were made of birch bark and used for holding berries. Basswood and tulip (whitewood) strips were later made into thin "scaleboards" and bent into all sorts of clever shapes, forming boxes with lids and even some made in one piece. Basswood was the favorite box material because when it dried it was very light and could therefore be weighed along with the food it contained without appreciably increasing the weight.*

That night Jonathan told Sarah about the incident with the Raggies.

"I'm glad you did something for them," she said. "They are such unfortunate people. I am sorry we haven't more basswood to give them, but the way things are now, the wood is worth more than the berries."

"They live on berries and apples from the forest crabs and what woodchucks they can trap. I think I should tell them to take our orchard gleanings when we harvest. At least they can have the windfalls."

"Yes," said Sarah, "that's a good idea. When it's time for them to gather apples, let them come to our orchard."

"But so few of the Raggies can speak English; it will be difficult to explain it to them. We can't have them helping themselves to all of our apples—let's give them all the apples from just one tree. Maybe from the old one that's about to fall apart. It still bears well."

"That's our old Seek-no-further!" said Sarah. "But do what you think best, Jonathan."

"I shall make a sign—'*Gift to the Raggies.*' I guess they can read that.

* *The Shakers, who specialized in making things of wood, made round and oval boxes that seem to outlast metal. There are still herb, pill, and spice boxes stronger now (through seasoning) than they were a century ago; their metal counterparts have become rusted and been discarded. The Shakers used elm, maple, and oak in their boxes, but considered basswood too fragile. The "fingers" or lap ends of Shaker boxes usually turn to the right because of a religious belief in the word "right" which made the Shakers shun anything going toward the left. It was contrary to order to kneel on the left knee first, to put on the left boot first, or to step first with the left foot. Their furniture was a masterpiece of "right angles."*

Then I'll just print 'Seek-no-further.' Maybe they will know what that means, too."

"It's a funny name!" said Sarah. "I wish I knew what it meant."

We do therefore . . . dedicate and solemnly devote this tree to be a Tree of Liberty. May all our councils and deliberations under its branches be guided by wisdom and directed to the support and maintenance of that liberty which our renowned forefathers sought out and found under trees and in the wilderness.

from a Dedication to a Tree of Liberty
Providence, Rhode Island.

1765

The Warehouse

In October of 1765, a group of American merchants met under a "Liberty Tree" and agreed that certain articles should not be brought into this country from England. There were many such trees, placed as monuments to spirit and patriotism, and designated as sites for meetings and the signing of charters. As John Adams commented in his diary, "In the course of this year, there have been innumerable monuments erected in the several colonies and provinces." What better monument to America, as an emblem of its God-given independence, than a tree? It was at this meeting in 1765 that the word "independence" took on a special and widespread meaning.

"With our land's wealth," said one Boston merchant, "we can all afford to be independent. There is probably nothing a man needs that we cannot make or grow in America. Look about you! Except for a piece of silk here and there, the clothes on our backs and every stick in our houses is American. We can be, indeed we *are*, the most independent people on earth!"

Those days, when the nation was struggling to be born, were perhaps our most poignant times, for it was an era when each man was forced to live with piercing intensity and perception. Two centuries later, when an American turns on the water and the lights in his apartment, he has little awareness of where these things come from; the greatest pity, however, is that he says, "Who cares where it comes from, as long as it keeps on coming?"

In 1765 everything a man owned was made more valuable by the fact that he had made it himself or knew exactly from where it had come. This is not so remarkable as it sounds; it is less strange that the eighteenth-century man should have a richer and keener enjoyment of life through knowledge than that the twentieth-century man should lead an arid and empty existence in the midst of wealth and extraordinary material benefits.

That century of magnificent awareness preceding the Civil War was the age of wood. Wood was not accepted simply as the material for building a new nation—it was an inspiration. Gentle to the touch, exquisite to contemplate, tractable in creative hands, stronger by weight than iron, wood was, as William Penn had said, "a substance with a soul." It spanned rivers for man; it built his home and heated it in the winter; man walked on wood, slept in it, sat on wooden chairs at wooden tables, drank and ate the fruits of trees from wooden cups and dishes. From cradle of wood to coffin of wood, the life of man was encircled by it.

One of the remarkable things about wood is its self-expression. Whether as the handle of a tool, as a dead stump, or alive in a forest where every branch is a record of the winds that blew, it is always telling something about itself. This is why man has an affinity with wood not only as a mere material, but also as a kindred spirit to live with and to know. The children of a century ago were expert at knowing trees and their characteristics; they grew up thinking of trees as having human qualities and, almost Druidlike, they tried to acquire the qualities of trees. A man might be as "strong as an oak," or "bend like a willow"; if he had

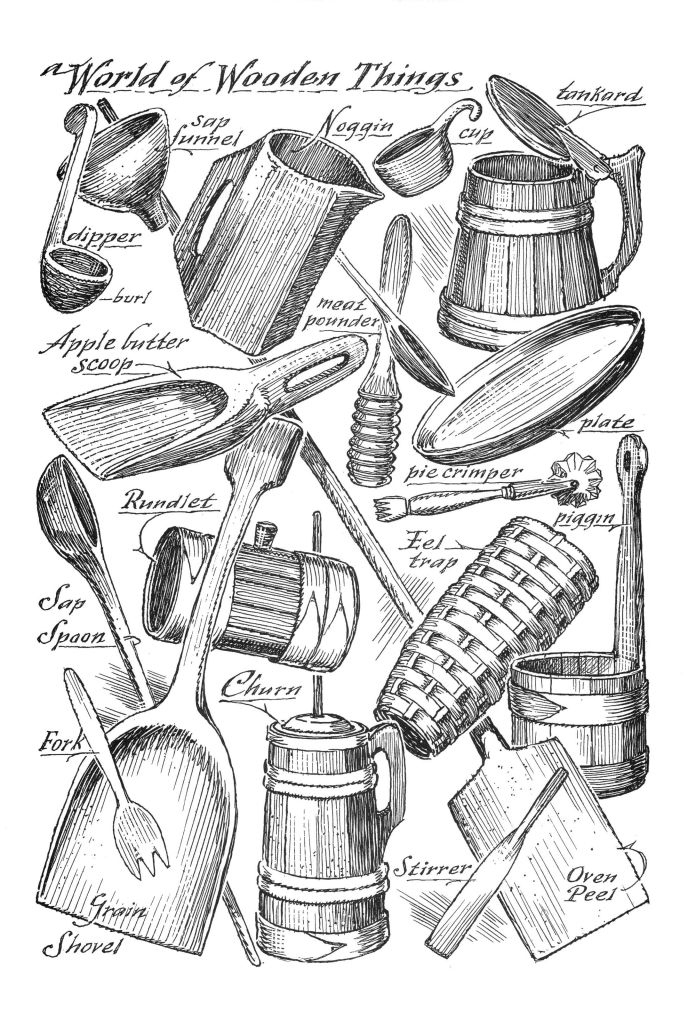

a World of Wooden Things

tankard

sap funnel

Noggin

cup

dipper

burl

meat pounder

Apple butter scoop

plate

pie crimper

Rundlet

Eel trap

piggin

Sap Spoon

Churn

Fork

Stirrer

Oven Peel

Grain Shovel

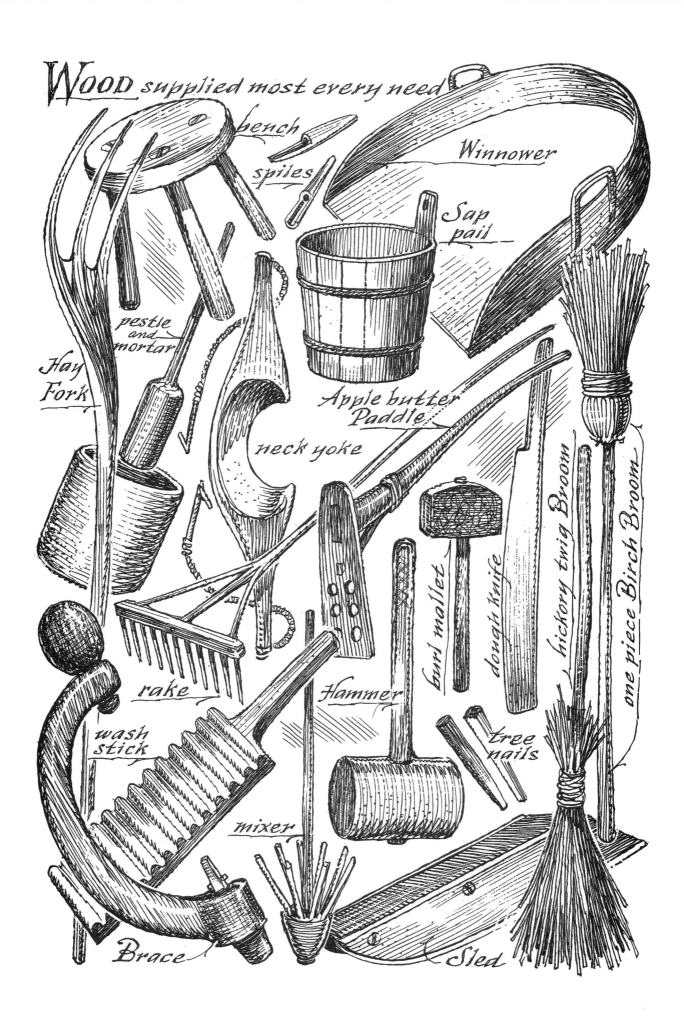

WOOD supplied most every need

bench

spiles

Winnower

Sap pail

pestle and mortar

Hay Fork

Apple butter Paddle

neck yoke

burl mallet

dough knife

hickory twig Broom

one piece Birch Broom

rake

Hammer

tree nails

wash stick

mixer

Brace

Sled

proper "timber," he'd become all the stronger from the winds of adversity.

The woodshed was an important part of the early American school, and so were the "horn books" or slabs of wood that held lesson cards in place. Even the classroom "slate" was wooden at first, made from a wide pine board painted a dull black. Even now, we still call it a "black*board*," although it is made of slate or plastic.

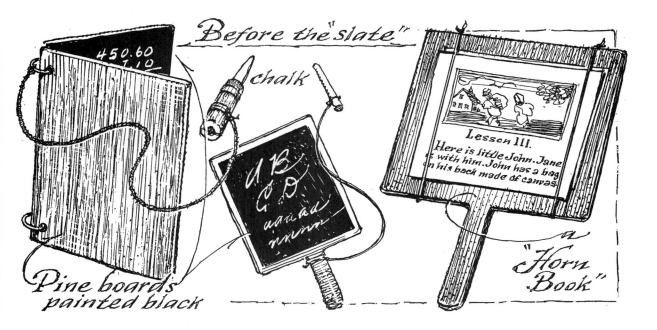

So it can be seen that in the pioneer days, everyone accepted wood in a way that we do not today. We can see why the early American's attitude toward the forest was reverent, and why when the colonies sought an emblem of independence for their flags, it was a tree. When they sought a symbol for the first coinage, the Massachusetts Bay Colony also chose the tree; the Pine Tree shilling along with the Willow Tree and Oak Tree coins seemed perfectly to symbolize America. Their designer, Joseph Jenks, said "What better thing than a tree, to portray the wealth of our country?"

In 1765 Benjamin Dean considered himself a rich man, although he had little money. He had bought half of his father's mill and some of the

"Bunker Hill Flag"

"Continental Flag"

AN APPEAL TO HEAVEN
Washington's Cruisers

LIBERTY TREE
AN APPEAL TO GOD
"Liberty Tree Flag"

Vermont Flag

DONT TREAD ON ME
Massachusetts (navy)

"these were once American Flags!"

MASATHVSETS
and this our first coin

New England Symbol.

Cornwall acreage that went with it: the Connecticut countryside had offered him everything that a pioneer American could wish for. His father, Reuben Dean, had, in his own words, "knocked down three score of trees and piled them into a serviceable house." And when that was done, he'd made use of the stream nearby and had gone about building the machinery for grinding. The first mill wheel was a small one with only enough power for grinding bark and herbs for the making of dyes and medicines. The recipes of "Doctor Reuben" had come from such sources as the Scatacook Indians, and his warehouse was no more than the surrounding forests. Chestnut-oak made a dark yellowish tan that most Cornwall women used for dying their woolens. Birch bark made an oil for perfume, and it also produced a lovely yellow dye; butternut made a deep brown. Tulip tree bark made a rich golden color, and Norway maple made a rosy tan. The ink used at Cornwall school came from pitch-pine lampblack and butternut juice. A good furniture stain was made from red oak bark, and if you wanted to make your own paint, you could get the best linseed oil base when Doc Reuben ground flax seed.

But he earned the name of "doctor" by his medicinal concoctions. He ground native holly bark for the relief of the ague. Fever bush or fever root were also cures. There was swamp laurel for diarrhea, slippery elm for a sore throat, black elder for skin infections, bayberry for dysentery, and ground aspen bark made a good substitute for quinine. The fine tan-colored "sawdust" left by the lyctus beetle (powder-post beetle) was collected and used as a baby powder. When spring came and tonics were in order, people asked for the essences and bark powders for sassafras and spice teas, birch beer, root beer, maple beer, and spruce beer. Doctor Reuben Dean's warehouse had an almost inexhaustible supply of remedies, and his mill was seldom silent.

Son Benjamin, however, had other interests. He had always enjoyed the sight of a blade passing through good wood; his nose was delighted by the tang of fresh sawdust and his ears tingled at the whine and clatter of sawmill machinery. His father had been content to copy the water wheels he'd seen and he'd never studied the mechanics of water power or the mathematical equations of power application. These were things for a younger mind. Hence, when Benjamin took over, his mind raced with the expectation of a bigger and better mill that would saw heavy timber, perhaps having gang saws so that a number of floor boards could be cut at the same time. He even knew what he intended to do with the sawdust and chips. He'd seen the new icehouses people were building, with

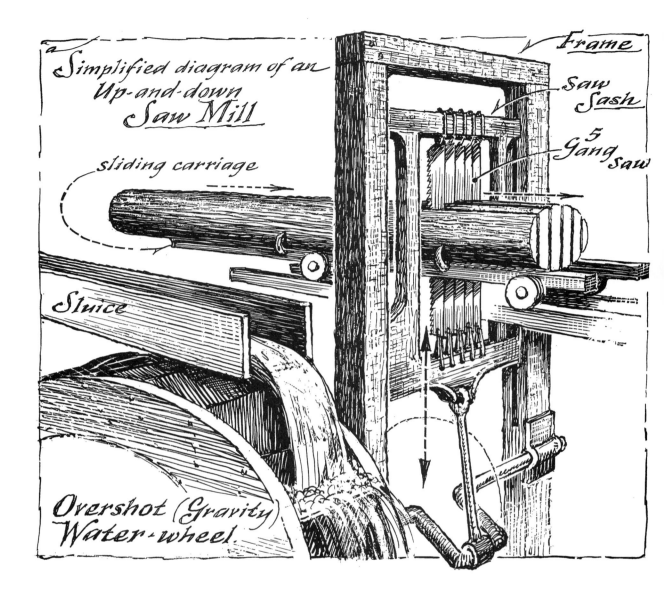

a Simplified diagram of an Up-and-down Saw Mill

sliding carriage

Frame

Saw Sash

5 Gang Saw

Sluice

Overshot (Gravity) Water-wheel.

charcoal-filled walls to preserve the ice; he felt certain that sawdust would work even better.

People were riving panel boards and wall sheathing by hand, so sawn boards should sell quickly, particularly those the width of the Cornwall pines—perhaps twenty to thirty inches. English homes had been traditionally walled with oak, but the colonial American home was usually wainscoted with pine. Not only was there an abundance of pine in America, but the wood had a soft and glowing patina and lavish widths of clear grain.

Wainscot has since become a misused word, for most people pronounce it "wains-coat" and they believe it refers to a wall-lining of wood at chair-rail height. Actually, it is a word taken from "wagenscot" (wagon-panel) and it is still to be pronounced the old way (like "wains-kut"). Some ridicule this Maine pronunciation, not realizing that the pronunciation is correct. Wainscoting means any wooden wall-lining, whether it be sheathing or paneling, horizontal or vertical, floor-to-ceiling or chair-rail height.

A panel in the true sense of the word should look like the underside of a shallow bread pan. In fact, that is where the word came from. Nowadays we speak of "pine-wall paneling" in describing tongue and groove

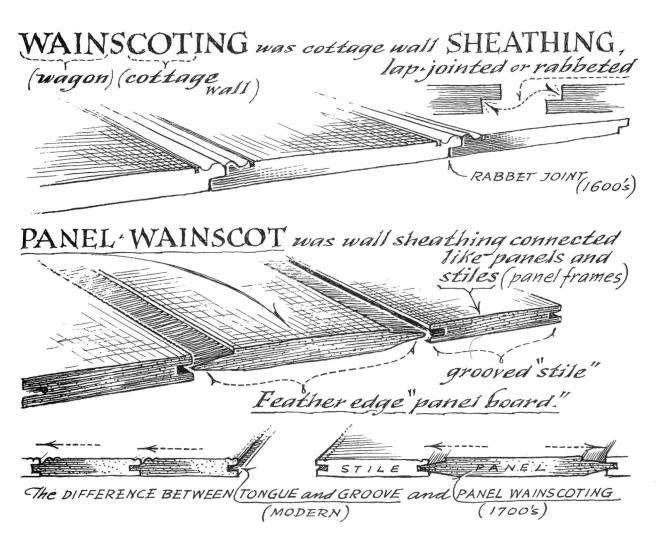

WAINSCOTING *was cottage wall* SHEATHING, *lap-jointed or rabbeted*
(wagon) (cottage wall)

RABBET JOINT (1600's)

PANEL·WAINSCOT *was wall sheathing connected like panels and stiles (panel frames)*

grooved "stile"

Feather edge "panel board."

STILE   PANEL

The DIFFERENCE BETWEEN TONGUE *and* GROOVE *and* PANEL WAINSCOTING
(MODERN)   (1700's)

79

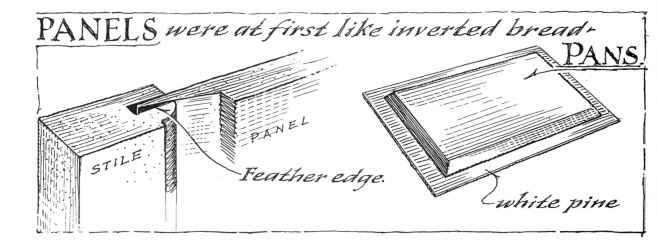

PANELS *were at first like inverted bread-* PANS

STILE

PANEL

Feather edge.

white pine

sheathing (or wainscoting). We also speak of "pumpkin pine" and some believe this is a kind of tree: pumpkin pine is merely ancient white pine. When new, it is tan-white, but softening and drying for over a century, it mellows into its pumpkinlike condition.*

Benjamin Dean's mill began to take form, and his household on nearby Dudleytown Hill saw him only at dinner and bedtime.

"As soon as we can," he told his wife, "I think we should sell this place and move into the valley near the mill."

"You can't work at the mill," said Ruth, "and still make the trip uphill each night. So move we shall, but I shall miss my orchard. It is just ready for its first good harvest."

"We shall have two orchards," said Benjamin. "The valley soil is thick with peat from prehistoric forests, and that will manure our orchard; it will grow the best eating apples."

"Then we shall leave the hilltop orchard for cider. It's taken hold now and needs just an occasional pruning."

And so it was. By the time the hilltop orchard had reached its peak, the Deans had moved into the valley next to the mill, and a new eating-apple orchard had been set out.

Planning an orchard in the 1700's was extremely exacting work, for apples were no occasional food. They were America's national food, and

* *Well-seasoned white pine was also known in New England as "apple pine."*

cider was the national drink. The first colonists had been instructed to drink as little water as possible. They had obeyed this dictum so well that even small children were brought up on teas and beers, and cider was served at every meal. In fact, there was apple at the table in some form all year round. So an apple orchard was planned to supply fresh eating apples and proper cooking apples for each season. Only the most poorly planned orchard would be in full bloom, with all the trees bearing at the same time. By proper planning and hastening or retarding ripening, an orchard might start its harvest period in summer and finish after the snow had arrived.

Scratching the bark of a fruit tree at certain times will hasten its bloom, and it was even a custom to shoot buckshot at an apple tree to help it bear in an "off year." Beating a tree's bark will bruise the layer just beneath it and check the descent of sap, forcing an early bearing. People used to beat fruit and nut trees with softwood clubs, and an old rhyme mentions this:

A woman, a watchdog, and a walnut tree,
The more you beat them the better they be.

There were tricks, too, in preserving eating apples. It started at picking time, when two men harvested each tree, using heavy gloves. No hand should touch the apple, and no two apples should rub against each other. The apple should be lifted upward to snap the stem off; if it were pulled, the stem would be ripped out of the apple and decay would start at once. Two apples at a time were handed down to a gloved packer who laid the apples carefully in straw (on a sled), and then covered them with a black cloth. A wheelbarrow or wagon jiggled too much, so a sled was used, and the apples were skidded over hay to the packing cellar. Sometimes they were packed in barrels; in that case the barrel was lifted by two men and walked to a sled. The man who was caught rolling a barrel of apples lost his job at once. "Watch a man gather apples," said one old almanac, "and you will see either a careful man or a careless man."

There were about two thousand well-known apples, and each one was

Picking Bag c.1790

Picking Ladder

scissors c.1860

SPLINT BASKET

Apple picker's "chair."

apple sled

Shaker device

X *sharp blades*

OPEN END

to be picked at a specific time for a specific purpose. The maturity of an apple was indicated by the condition of the seed, so one apple was opened and used as a test. Winter apples were picked when mature, yet not ripe; late winter apples were picked before the first good frost, but when they were just hard enough to withstand thumb pressure.

Eating apples were often placed on their sides in baked sawdust, or in well-dried timothy chaff. Noah Webster recommended packing apples in heat-dried sand. Most people hung their special apples "by their tails" (stems), and some packed them in grain. It was the custom when shipping apples overseas to ship grain at the same time; in this way apples

82

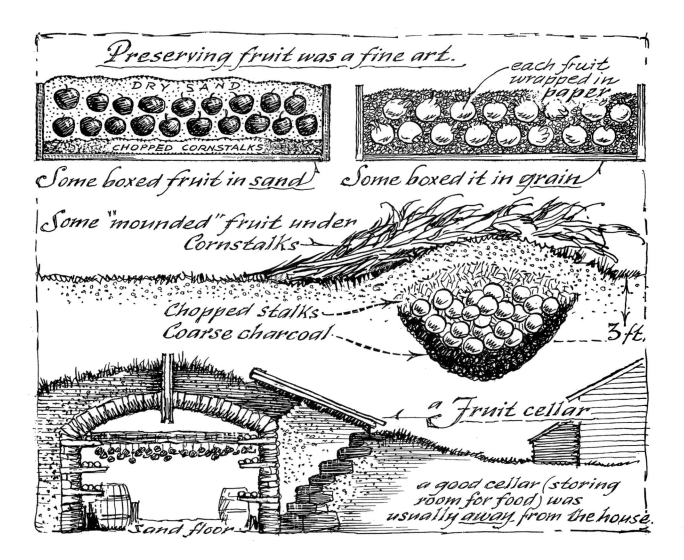

Preserving fruit was a fine art.

DRY SAND

CHOPPED CORNSTALKS

each fruit wrapped in paper

Some boxed fruit in sand *Some boxed it in grain*

Some "mounded" fruit under Cornstalks

Chopped stalks
Coarse charcoal

3 ft.

"Fruit cellar"

a good cellar (storing room for food) was usually away from the house.

Sand floor

could be packed in with the grain. Marble shelves were popular in the Vermont and Connecticut apple cellars, as they kept the apples cold and dry. Some had windmills that operated fans to keep the air moving (thus retarding spoilage), but every housewife knew enough to fan the air each time she went to the storage room. There are reports of apples correctly packed or hung in the "correct atmosphere" that have kept for more than two years.

Perhaps no tree has given America more of itself than the apple tree. Besides its vinegars and medicines, we might recall apple duff, apple brandy, applejack, apple dowdy, also crowdy and dowler (pies), apple waffle, apple butter, apple cake, applesauce, apple leather (broiled and

. . By their tails.

dried apples), apple slump, candy apple, and numerous other examples of apple Americana. Its wood was used for machinery, particularly for cogs, wheels, and shuttles; whenever a spoon or stirrer was used for apple butter or sauce, applewood was the choice. Jonathan Chapman, who became known as Johnny Appleseed, said, "Nothing gives more yet asks less in return, than a tree; particularly the apple."

Whenever you walk in the forest and you come upon an apple tree, stop and look about. Very likely you will see several others, too. And perhaps some ancient, stunted lilac bushes. Nearby there will probably be the ruins of an ancient house foundation, a cellar where apples were once stored, kept throughout the winter, fresh for the table before the heat of summer. It is still like that on deserted Dudleytown Mountain near Cornwall. There, in about 1910 when the blight had already turned the first chestnut leaves brown, the last of the Dudleytown houses fell into its own cellar. People began talking about the "curse of Dudleytown" and history books told about this "deserted ghost town," with its eerie place names—Dark Entry Road and Owlsboro Lane.

Actually, there is no mystery about the place; its disappearance as a village was just part of a cycle. When people first moved there in the early 1700's, they settled on the high areas for their own protection. The lowlands were wet, covered with moss, and did not present inviting sites for homes. But within a half century, when the valleys were hunted and harvested and mills (which had to be near water) were established, the hilltop settlements were abandoned. Further, the hilltops have much less topsoil on them, and so they were "farmed out" quickly.

Remnants of the Dean hilltop orchard can still be found in the third growth of forest. If you stand where the Dean house was, you may be standing eight or ten feet above the old excavation floor, for the forest has a habit of building up a compost to cover old wounds. Near the site of the old house there is a pile of stones, which marks the end of a long-gone rail fence; there an old apple tree hulk remains rotting on the ground. But if you walk along its body, you will come to a live shoot, fed in some mysterious way by the fallen parent. The tree was upright when Benjamin Dean left for Ohio in 1810. Ruth remembered it well, for she took some of it with her—the only part of Cornwall which they didn't leave behind them.

She had bent a branch of the tree downward one midsummer, and after slicing through the tender bark so that some day it might root, she had inserted the branch into and through a pot of earth. For two seasons

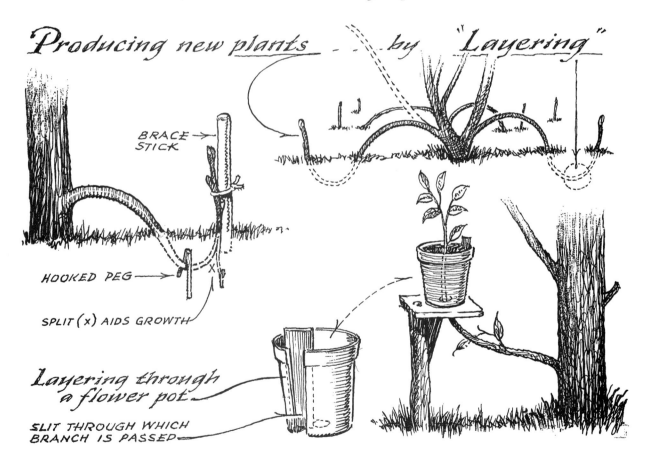

Producing new plants — *by* "*Layering*"

BRACE STICK →

HOOKED PEG →

SPLIT (x) AIDS GROWTH

Layering through a flower pot

SLIT THROUGH WHICH BRANCH IS PASSED

she had nursed the "layering pot," keeping it wrapped with cloths and watering it daily, until roots had emerged from the cut portion within the pot. When separated from the parent plant, it was put, pot and all, beneath the big tree, and Ruth had called it "mother watching over her baby." Benjamin enjoyed the spectacle, but when the time came to unearth the pot and transport it to Ohio, he rebelled.

"Why in the world," Benjamin had said, "do you want to carry that heavy box with you? Such a tiny tree will likely die on the long trip. Anyway, there are plenty of apple trees in Ohio."

"I know that," Ruth replied, "but women are sentimental and men forgive them. It's not such a heavy box, and I shall take care of watering and shading it till we get to Ohio. If the tree lives, it will be worth all the trouble. It will be taking some of our old place with us. It was our favorite tree—it came from England and it can make another historic trip."

"Very well," Benjamin consented. "It's a silly idea, and a silly name, too. Traveling across the country with a baby 'Seek-no-further'!"

In 1665 Harvard College graduated an American Indian named Cheeshahteaumuck.

The New World

For so young a nation, it is strange that the beginnings of America should be so shrouded in mythical legend. Any schoolboy will tell you that Betsy Ross designed the Stars and Stripes and that the Pilgrims were the first settlers to step on the shores of New England (on Plymouth Rock, in fact).

Actually, when the Pilgrims sailed for our shores they had an extraordinarily good map of New England and more travel literature than one might expect. The map they used was made a half-dozen years before, and it showed such names as Boston, Hull, Dartmouth, Cambridge, Norwich, Southampton, Ipswich, Oxford, and Sandwich. Oh, yes—there was also a place named *Plimouth!*

Of course there were other maps of the New England territory, for by 1620 there were many fishing stations in Maine. That year a Maine gristmill had sent a shipload of grain to England, and three years before, Pocahontas had died in London. This rather explodes the schoolboy picture of the New England coast as an unexplored land of savage Indians.

Among the Indians that the Pilgrims met were those who spoke English. "Welcome! Welcome, Englishmen!" said Samoset. "But wait—I shall get Squanto who was educated in London. I am sure he will speak better English than I."

When the new Verrazano Bridge, connecting Brooklyn and Staten Island, was built, there were very few schoolboys who had ever heard the name. Yet a century before the Plymouth Plantation was established, a gentleman named Verrazano described the New England coast: "We found another land high ful of thicke woods," he wrote. "The trees were of firres, cipresses and such like are wont to grow in cold Countreys." He suffered from poor publicity, it seems, for his accounts are seldom mentioned; Cartier did a little better. As he went up the New England coast, he wrote about the "pleasant countrey full of all sorts of goodly trees, Ceders, Firres, Ashes, Boxe and Willowes." Captain John Smith is well known for his romantic exploits, but his impressions of the New World had more talk about wood in them than anything else. "The treasures of this land," he wrote, "have never been opened, nor her originalls wasted, consumed or abused . . . overgrown with all sorts of excellent woodes for the building of houses, boats, barks or shippes." It is interesting that unlike European maps, all the early maps of America have trees drawn upon them. And with the slightest research, it is easy to see that the New World was not one of "freedom" so much as it was a gigantic warehouse of wood.

In the spring of 1665 a ship lay in Bristol Harbor, ready for journeying to the New World. Its hold was full of cargo for the people of Massachusetts. But by making the most of their new-found wealth, the colonists had become largely self-sufficient in four decades, and British merchants were hard pressed to find goods to entice the American taste. Glass, nail-rods, silks, teas, and spices took up very little room and weight, so English bricks were added to ballast the ship in case of a rough sea. The colonists were making good brick already and had little need of bricks from Britain, but as they were sold at a loss on this side of the ocean, they were always welcome. No need for ballast on the way back, for chestnut and oak and hickory have good weight.

The ship was not a new one; it had made the crossing almost a hundred times, mostly as a sassafras carrier. It was one of a fleet of its kind—the *Susan Constant*, the *Discoverer*, and the *Treasurer* (which had carried Sir Thomas Dale and Pocahontas from America to England).

Sassafras is a tree very closely associated with America, although few are now aware of its history. As the early American wonder drug, it was our first money crop and object-in-trade of the first American cartel. In 1622 the Jamestown Colony was committed by the Crown to produce thirty tons of sassafras, with a penalty of ten pounds of tobacco on each man who did not produce one hundred pounds of it.

Sassafras was supposed to cure almost any ailment; used as a tea or a tonic it became the favorite drink of England. And when rumor started that sassafras retarded old age, the sassafras trade reached its peak.

No cure-all has had better publicity than sassafras. Its popularity began

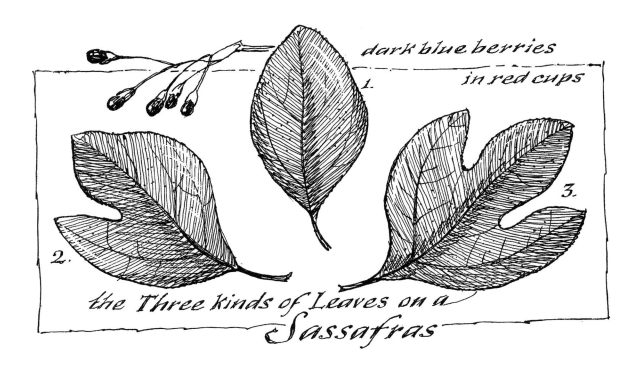

dark blue berries
in red cups
1.

2.

3.

the Three kinds of Leaves on a Sassafras

with the writings of Doctor Nicolas Monardes in 1569. "It healeth opila-tions," he wrote, "it comforteth the liver and stomach and doth disopi-late; to give appetite to eat; in the headache, in griefes of the stomach; it causeth to cast out gravel and stones; it removeth the impediments that cause barrenness and maketh women to conceave; in the toothache; in the evil of the poxe and eville of the joints." Then an incident occurred in Roanoke that really captured the public imagination: it concerned a group of Virginians who had traveled far beyond the camp where their food was stored and were, therefore, reduced to eating their dogs, cooked in a soup of sassafras. When their dogs were all eaten, the Virginians lived on sassafras soup alone, which was reported to give them a strange new vitality.

When Sir Francis Drake visited Roanoke in 1586 and brought some of the half-starved colonists back with him, he also brought back a load of sassafras, livened by the tale of the "wondrous root which kept the starving alive and in fair goode spirit."

The smell and taste of sassafras is unlike any other spice, and legend has it that the odor alone will keep away sickness and evil, as well as vermin. Spoons were often made of sassafras wood, cradles were inlaid with it, noggins of sassafras added extra flavor to a drink, and Bible boxes were made of the wood to keep away evil spirits. It was said that a ship with sufficient sassafras wood in her hull would never be wrecked. Indeed, the ship at Bristol had fared well; the pungent odor of sassafras still per-meated her holds.

The ship's master, Robert Carter, was dining at the estate of Ralph Austin, "an extraordinary practicer in ye art of planting." The dinner had been a bon voyage meeting, for Robert Carter was to leave on the next tide. The time for fruit and brandy had come.

"I envy you your journey," said the host, "and drink Godspeed to you. You will reach America at Goose Summer, and the harvesting will be at its peak; it will be an exciting and colorful spectacle."

"In America they call it Indian Summer," said Carter, "and indeed there is color such as we never see in England. They say the first frost sets the leaves afire, and from then on a man can look at the hills and tell by the colors what kinds of trees are there. The browns and tans are hickory, the yellows are tulip and beech and ironwood; the black gum and oak and maple turn flaming red, while the purples are the leaves of white and mountain ash."

"They say that the orange colors are so bright they hurt your eyes."

"Yes, they do—those are the leaves of sassafras and sugar maple."

"And when you arrive in America," said Ralph Austin, "I hope that you will remember to gather what information you can about the orchards there. The plague of ice that struck us here in England last year must surely have killed many orchard trees; only the most hardy can have survived. I shall want grafts and layers of them for England. And you must keep accounts for me, telling me of all the astounding trees of the New World."

"I shall do this indeed," said Robert, "but I am of the opinion that many of the American trees would not survive the temperate mildness of the air of Britain—they seem to need the intense atmospheric changes of America. Birch, for example, has been known to grow in England for centuries, yet nothing like the American birch has ever been seen here. The Indians choose one large birch tree and make two cuts down its trunk on opposite sides; then they make two encircling cuts at top and bottom. In the spring when the bark is peeling, the Indians lift away these two curled pieces of bark and sew them together to make a boat which they call a 'canoo.'"

"Remarkable!" said Ralph Austin. "And what do they use for sewing?"

"Again a tree! They use the roots of the white spruce, and to make the boat watertight they heat the wood of balsam fir until its resin oozes out and they mix it with the pitch of pine. But the biggest 'canoos' are the ones made of solid wood. There is tale of one made from a hollowed sycamore that is sixty-five feet long and carries nine thousand pounds. In America the old sycamore usually has a hollow trunk, and great barrels are made with the slightest effort. Even well-linings are made from these hollow

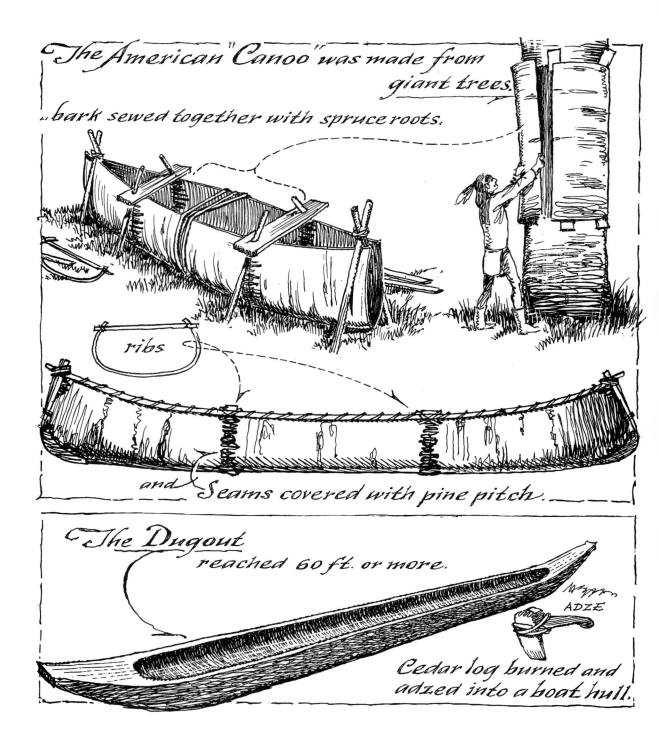

The American "Canoo" was made from giant trees.

...bark sewed together with spruce roots.

ribs

and Seams covered with pine pitch.

The Dugout reached 60 ft. or more.

ADZE

Cedar log burned and adzed into a boat hull.

sycamore trunks, and sometimes they are used as storage bins, as big around as an armspread and a perch in height."

"This very year," he continued, "a mast was felled in Maine which

SYCAMORE *hollow trunks made storage bins*

and tubs — *and cisterns*

and all sorts of Containers

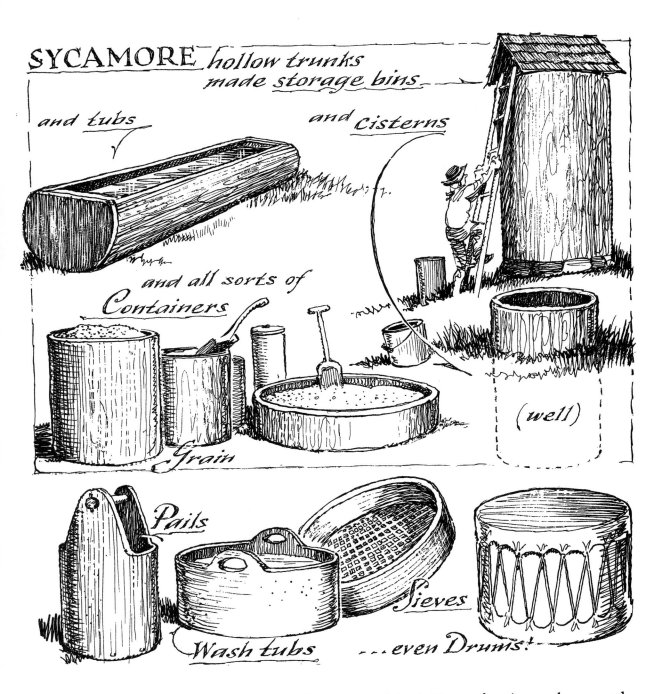

(well)

Grain

Pails

Wash tubs

Sieves

...even Drums!

proved too big for any of our mast ships.* Even after it was hewn and shaped, it had a useable length of one hundred and thirty feet and

---

* There were special ships for carrying mast material for the British Navy. They were bargelike and had long, uninterrupted floors that could hold hundred-foot lengths. The masts were slid through a door in the stern, and the largest mast ship could hold fifty masts. Pine trees more than two foot in diameter (three feet from the ground) were reserved for masts for the Royal Navy, and the "Broad Arrow Mark" was placed on tree trunks by Royal Tree Viewers, marking them as British property.

weighed over twenty-five tons. Why, there are pines in Massachusetts that have no extending limbs until a hundred feet from the ground!"

"But these wonders are not what I can write about in these times," said Austin. "England is badly in need of timber because of the waste of its resources; we must implant the value of the growing tree and inspire the

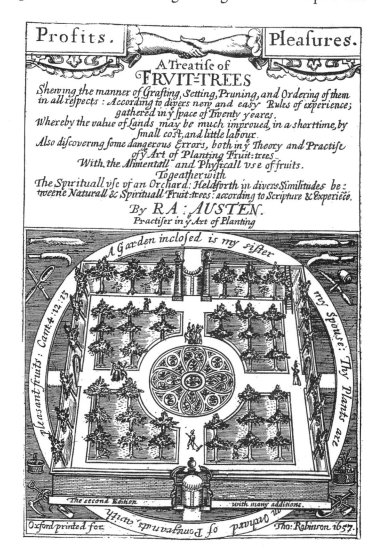

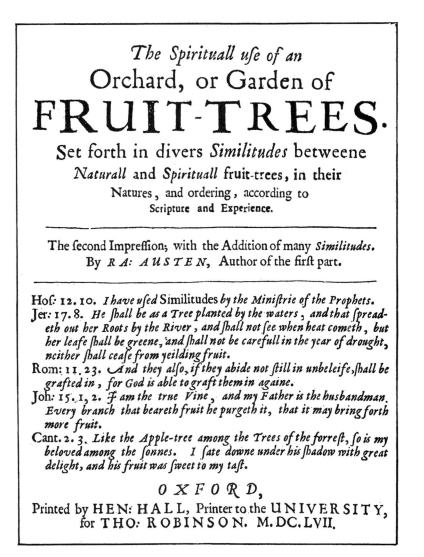

The Spirituall use of an
Orchard, or Garden of
FRUIT-TREES.
Set forth in divers *Similitudes* betweene
Naturall and *Spirituall* fruit-trees, in their
Natures, and ordering, according to
Scripture and Experience.

The second Impreſſion; with the Addition of many *Similitudes.*
By *RA: AUSTEN,* Author of the firſt part.

Hoſ: 12. 10. *I have uſed* Similitudes *by the Miniſtrie of the Prophets.*
Jer: 17. 8. *He ſhall be as a Tree planted by the waters, and that ſpread-
eth out her Roots by the River, and ſhall not ſee when heat cometh, but
her leafe ſhall be greene, and ſhall not be carefull in the year of drought,
neither ſhall ceaſe from yeilding fruit.*
Rom: 11. 23. *And they alſo, if they abide not ſtill in unbeleife, ſhall be
grafted in, for God is able to graft them in againe.*
Joh: 15. 1, 2. *I am the true Vine, and my Father is the husbandman.
Every branch that beareth fruit he purgeth it, that it may bring forth
more fruit.*
Cant. 2. 3. *Like the Apple-tree among the Trees of the forreſt, ſo is my
beloved among the ſonnes. I ſate downe under his ſhadow with great
delight, and his fruit was ſweet to my taſt.*

OXFORD,
Printed by HEN: HALL, Printer to the UNIVERSITY,
for THO: ROBINSON. M. DC. LVII.

farmer in a Godly way, so that he will plant and know the benefits of propagating timber trees and orchards."

"I have read your writings, good Ralph," said Robert, "and I can perhaps even quote you. 'The world is a great library, and fruit trees are some of the books wherein we may read and see plainly the attributes of God.' Perhaps America will need such a philosophy, too, before it wastes its trees, thinking of them as just so much material wealth. I shall take your book with me and show it to those who will read its wisdom."

Agriculture and husbandry during the 1600's and 1700's were not a business, but a way of life. This explains why writings about agriculture were so filled with Biblical quotations and moral philosophy. Austin, in speaking of pruning, for example, tells how fruit trees that spread widely and grow low near the ground bear more and larger fruit than high trees, and the fruit is easier to reach. This might be forgotten by the reader, except for the typical religious application as he writes, ". . . and humble Christians, too, bring forth more and fairer fruit than lofty persons, while their acts are easier to reach."

A servant entered with a tray of nuts and fruits, and Austin passed them to his guest.

"England's orchards of forest trees are most depleted. Some of the boat builders are using fruitwoods, as are the joiners. Nothing is wasted now, but it is almost too late. The ship *Mayflower* is now the beams and rafters of a barn in Buckingham. Whatever new wood we need for our navy will come from the New World."

Robert Carter broke an apple in two, admired its meat, and sprinkled it with cinnamon spice. "It is time for me to leave," he said. "I should like to take one of these fine apples with me and plant the seed in America."

"What a fine idea! But the seed would not propagate that same apple, and a graft might not last the voyage. But wait! I shall get you a layering plant, and you shall be the first to bring my prize across the ocean. I have worked a long time to create this variety; I have not named it yet. I would be pleased for you to name it. Perhaps the 'Westfield,' after your farm in Massachusetts? Perhaps it might be named after your ship! What is the name of your ship?"

"It is called the *Seek-no-further*."

a compact description for recognizing a few of the typical American Trees

On the following pages—not alphabetically listed or at all complete—are illustrated a random selection of trees that might be seen in a stroll through the countryside. Points of recognition—leaf shapes, cones, coloring, size—as the author knows them, are shown in the sketches and explained in the text, thus identifying the woods pictured in the color insert at the beginning of the book.

Just as it is possible to recognize certain people in a crowd by the way they stand or act, it is also possible to identify a tree—even at some distance—by its size, color, or shape. Some trees grow in small groups within the forest, while others mass together and crowd out everything that is unlike themselves. There are stunted trees that grow in poor soil, and there are towering beauties that mark places of rich soil. The aspen leaf quivers in the wind, the oak leaf whips about, and the beech and maple leaves turn over. Each kind of tree has its own movement or manner of growing that is just as interesting to note as the scientific properties given in a precise tree guidebook.

Grotesque, stately, vaselike, prim, solemn, rugged—these are the words a woodsman uses in describing trees, though he probably does not know their scientific names. It is the woodsman's point of view that is employed in the text and represented in the illustrations on the pages that follow.

SYCAMORE (Buttonball and/or Buttonwood)—is easily recognized by its bark which resembles "old scraped-off wall paper." The trunks of mature sycamores are often hollow; their limbs are remarkably light in color, ranging from cream to gray, pale green, and tan. The fruit is a ball of seeds.

TULIP TREE (yellow poplar or whitewood)—an outstanding tree in the forest, it has a magnificent straight trunk and neatly furrowed gray bark. It is not really a poplar, though many country people call it "popple." Its flower is like a tulip; its fruit a cone of many winged seeds.

CHESTNUT—has disappeared from the American forest except as a small tree that rises from old blighted stumps to a height of about ten feet before it, in turn, succumbs to the blight. The leaves are very long, prominently veined, and sharp-toothed.

AMERICAN ELM—flares up and outward in a vaselike fashion. Its wood, difficult to split, was used for ship blocks, wheel hubs, and yokes; its bark was used for cord and for chair bottoms. The SLIPPERY elm leaf is larger than that of the American elm, but has smaller teeth, and is rough all over the bottom. This tree is not as tall and is less vaselike in appearance than the American or white elm.

AMERICAN ASH—has leaves set opposite each other on the twigs. Recognizing the different varieties of ash trees is difficult for there are red, white, blue, green, black, and yellow ashes. Shown opposite are the two most valuable kinds— American (or white) ash and black ash. All of the ash trees have a single winged seed. Ash *bends* with supreme strength, but since it *splits* with precision, splints for baskets, chairs, and hoops were made from the black variety. Blue ash produced a dye from its inner bark, and its wood made superior pitchfork handles. White ash was second in value to oak, being the best material for tool handles, oars, and for any implement where elasticity and strength were required.

SYCAMORE
has limbs like a Javanese dancer's arms and Bark like torn wall paper

BUTTON·BALL FRUIT

TULIP TREE

MOST LIKELY TULIPS

NO POINT AT END OF LEAF

fruit CLOSED OPEN

flower

CHESTNUT

STILL TRYING TO GROW

American ELM *can be recognized by its shape*

"ONE SIDED" LEAF

Slippery Elm leaf is bigger

thin waferlike seeds

WHITE or AMERICAN ELM

American ASH *(white ash)*

LEAF HAS FAIRLY LONG STEM: OTHER ASHES HAVE LESS OR NO STEM

BARK ASH GRAY

Black Ash

WHITE ASH SEED

BARK FURROWS SELDOM CROSS

seed *wing*

BLACK CHERRY—a valuable timber tree, is prized by cabinetmakers. Because it can be polished to a deep and glowing red, many of the finest early table tops and interior panels were made of cherry wood. Varying from shrubs ten feet tall to trees one hundred feet high, black cherry is often plagued by rot, tent caterpillars, and other insects. The young tree has beautiful, reddish, smooth bark with conspicuous horizontal marks. As the tree ages, the bark becomes black (like pine) and, starting at the bottom, cracks off in thin brittle scales. Pin cherry and sweet cherry are small trees. Choke cherry is even smaller—really only a shrub—and bears an unpalatable dark red berry.

AMERICAN HOLLY—is the best known of about fifteen varieties of holly. It reaches about twenty to fifty feet in height, with nearly horizontal limbs and an ash-gray bark, somewhat like beech. Its wood is compact with a satiny texture, and is used for wood engraving, inlay work, screws, and tool handles.

WALNUT—a most valuable hardwood, has leaves that are fine-toothed, pointed, smooth above and hairy beneath. There are from fifteen to twenty-three leaves on a black walnut branch and from eleven to nineteen leaves on a white walnut (butternut) branch. Black walnut has a darker bark and its round nut grows in a thick green husk. The butternut spreads more and has lighter, grayer bark and slightly broader, more hairy leaves. Husks from both of these walnuts produce a fine yellow dye. Black walnut was used in making water wheels and as charcoal for gunpowder. Sugar was produced from the sap of the butternut.

LIVE OAK—symbol of the Southland, this tree spreads tremendously. Its leaves are somewhat like those of the laurel and willow oak, but are more elliptical, blunt-tipped, and leathery, and are green throughout the year. The wood of the oak is valued for hardness, strength, and durability.

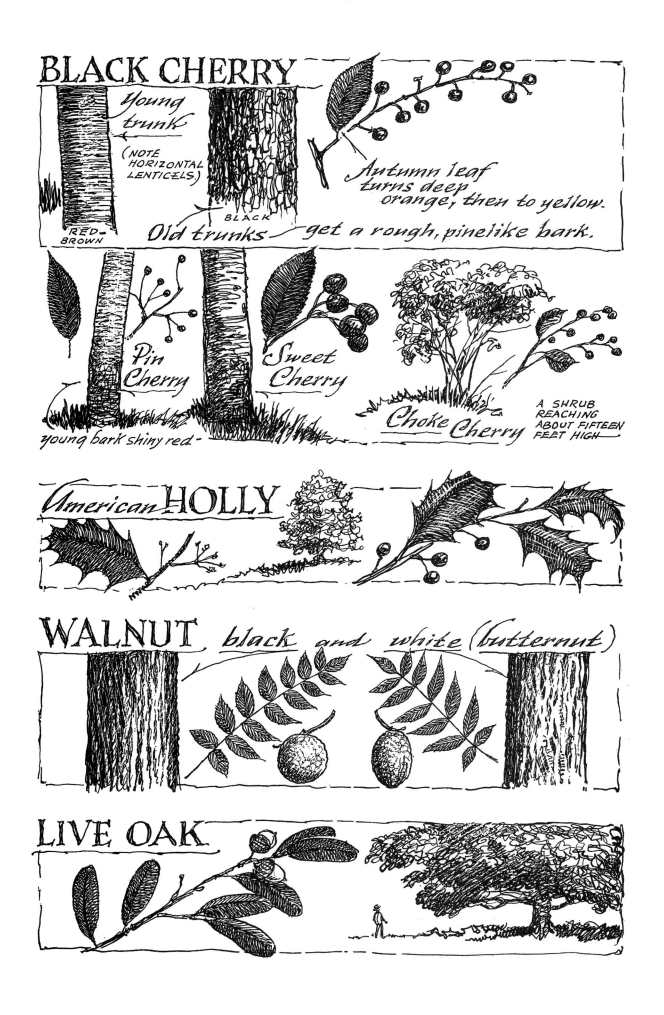

BLACK CHERRY

Young trunk (NOTE HORIZONTAL LENTICELS.)

RED-BROWN

BLACK

Old trunks get a rough, pinelike bark.

Autumn leaf turns deep orange, then to yellow.

Pin Cherry

young bark shiny red –

Sweet Cherry

Choke Cherry

A SHRUB REACHING ABOUT FIFTEEN FEET HIGH

American HOLLY

WALNUT *black and white (butternut)*

LIVE OAK

HICKORY—can be recognized by the three large top leaves on its compound branch. The SHAGBARK variety has brittle bark, a straight, narrow trunk, and vertical fissures. The fruits of the PIGNUT and MOCKERNUT (not shown) resemble each other, and the bark of each is somewhat similar to the pattern of walnut bark. Hickory wood is an excellent fuel that burns brightly, and during Colonial days it was used in most hearths for both warmth and illumination. In tensile strength, hickory is on a par with wrought iron. In autumn, the tree's dress turns to many beautiful shades of yellow.

BIRCHES—are readily identified by the tissue-paper quality of their bark and caterpillarlike catkin flower. CANOE (paper) birch grows to one hundred feet or more and has oval leaves. WHITE (gray) birch usually grows in thickets and reaches only about thirty feet in height. BLACK birch has aromatic twigs, and a tighter, blackish, less papery bark that is inclined to crack in a downward direction. It is often mistaken for black cherry. YELLOW birch grows as tall as one hundred feet and has bark that peels into yellow-silver strips. RED birch, found near streams, has a loosely peeling, shaggy, reddish bark.

AMERICAN BEECH—a stately tree, has shiny, velvet-smooth gray bark. Its nuts are great favorites with animals and birds. The foliage has an iron-rust color in the autumn. HORNBEAM, a shrublike tree that grows under the larger trees in the forest, has what appear to be "muscles" along its black-gray trunk. Its other name, IRONWOOD, is descriptive of its quality—it is one of the strongest woods and hence excellent for levers and handles. HOP HORNBEAM (not shown) is a taller relation that grows from fifteen to twenty-five feet high and, like the elm, its bark has vertical scales.

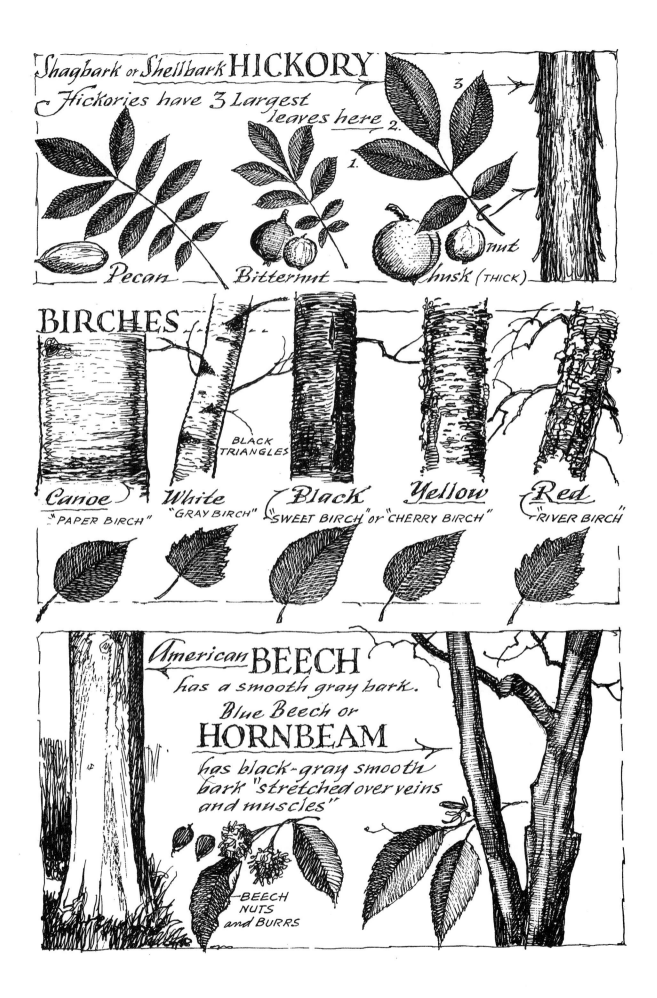

Shagbark or Shellbark HICKORY
Hickories have 3 Largest leaves here

3
2.
1.

Pecan   Bitternut   nut
husk (THICK)

BIRCHES

BLACK TRIANGLES

Canoe   White   Black   Yellow   Red
"PAPER BIRCH"   "GRAY BIRCH"   "SWEET BIRCH" or "CHERRY BIRCH"   "RIVER BIRCH"

American BEECH
has a smooth gray bark.
Blue Beech or
HORNBEAM
has black-gray smooth bark "stretched over veins and muscles"

BEECH NUTS and BURRS

MAPLE—all varieties bear two buds, directly opposite each other on a twig. From these twin buds come twin branches and twin leaves. The leaves and twigs are adjacent, but usually extend away from each other. Properly called samara, the fruit of the maple, because of the way it hangs in clusters, is also referred to as "keys" or key fruit. In autumn, the maple trees put on a brilliant show of colors, making recognition easy—even at a distance. Bird's-eye and curly maple are not distinct varieties, but rather are common maple with grain irregularities that give them these names.

SUGAR MAPLE (also known as Rock Maple and Hard Maple)—has bark that becomes —with age—deeply furrowed, gray, scaly, and brittle. Its leaf is about as long as it is wide; its limbs grow upward and outward. NORWAY maple has a leaf similar to the sugar maple, but it is wider than it is long. This, and also a milky juice that can be seen when the leaf stem is broken, distinguish it from sugar maple.

MOUNTAIN MAPLE (Dwarf Maple)—is shrublike with small-toothed leaves and gray bark. STRIPED maple (Moosewood) is another midget-sized maple. Its trunk is a dark green, striped with white; its leaf is large and round-bottomed.

SILVER MAPLE (White Maple)—this large tree is distinguished by its deeply cut leaves. Its keys are very long, with one wing of this fruit often shorter than the other. The leaves of the silver maple turn a dull yellow in the fall season. SYCAMORE maple is also called "False Sycamore" in the United States; in Europe it is known only as the sycamore. It, too, has key fruit that clings to the twigs throughout winter, and its buds remain green. The bark breaks off in small squares, making its trunk resemble that of the American sycamore and thus accounting for the name.

RED MAPLE—has some red color through all seasons of the year. In spring, the buds are red; in summer, the keys ripen to a deep shade of red and the leafstalks and veins remain red; and this maple is the first tree to turn red in the autumn. The ASH-LEAF maple (box elder) is an exceptional maple with compound leaves. It is valuable as a shade tree because of the rapid rate at which it grows.